MW00980430

THE CHRÉTIEN LEGACY

A CANADIAN'S VIEW

of the administration of

THE RIGHT HONOURABLE

JEAN CHRÉTIEN

PRIME MINISTER OF
CANADA

1993 - 2003

by

Jack Dixon

Note for Librarians: a cataloguing record for this book that includes Dewey Classification and US Library of Congress numbers is available from the National Library of Canada. The complete cataloguing record can be obtained from the National Library s online database at:
www.nlc-bnc.ca/amicus/index-e.html

ISBN 1-4120-2166-9

TRAFFORD

This book was published on-demand in cooperation with Trafford Publishing.
On-demand publishing is a unique process and service of making a book available for retail sale to the public taking advantage of on-demand manufacturing and Internet marketing. On-demand publishing includes promotions, retail sales, manufacturing, order fulfilment, accounting and collecting royalties on behalf of the author.

Suite 6E, 2333 Government St., Victoria, B.C. V8T 4P4, CANADA
Phone   250-383-6864   Toll-free   1-888-232-4444 (Canada & US)
Fax   250-383-6804   E-mail   sales@trafford.com
Web site www.trafford.com   TRAFFORD PUBLISHING IS A DIVISION OF TRAFFORD HOLDINGS LTD.
Trafford Catalogue #03-2715   www.trafford.com/robots/03-2715.html
10   9   8   7   6   5   4   3

THE

CHRÉTIEN

LEGACY

I see nothing quite conclusive in the art of temporal government,
But violence, duplicity, and frequent malversation.
King rules or baron rules.
The strong man strongly and the weak man by caprice.
They have but one law, to seize power and keep it,
And the steadfast can manipulate the greed and lust of others,
The feeble is devoured by his own.

> T.S. Eliot, *Murder in the Cathedral.*

"This is the negation of God into a system of government."

> Anon.

Yes, he's broadened out --
he's twice the man he was; a pity, though,
his life should run, like bright oil down a gutter,
to implement some politican's promise.

> Frederick Horn, *Conscript*

That one may smile, and smile, and be a villain.

> *Hamlet*

This booklet started out in the form of an open letter to Prime Minister Jean Chrétien, and was drafted in the idea that he was due to relinquish office in February 2004. Now that he has decided to step down in December 2003, it was decided to retain the format. There will undoubtedly be assessments and evaluations of his character, performance and administration. Lest some commentators be carried away on a wave of misplaced sympathy, the author has felt it important to publish an antidote to any such movement, and to ensure that his record of misdeeds and defects be taken into full account in any future history or biography.

I extend my grateful thanks to Angela Aidoo for her professional skill in the formatting of the text and pages of this booklet

I accuse you, Jean-Joseph CHRÉTIEN, of public conduct and political acts that combine to ensure that you are the worst prime minister that this country has ever had the misfortune of being saddled with. To say what I mean by 'the worst' is as easy as it is distressing. You are the most autocratic and bigoted politician ever to occupy a seat in the House of Commons; and your policies, whenever you have been forced, with acute reluctance, to pronounce policies, as well as your lack of policies in crucial areas of public affairs, have brought grievous harm to Canada's former good name in the eyes of other nations and peoples; to our national security and defences; and to our society and our people in their striving to better their lives and to live together in a common respect and harmony. Moreover-and this charge is worse by far -if the many sources and accounts that all Canadians have read in the past several years about your conduct as a politician and Prime Minister are true, you are the most corrupt politician ever to have sullied the profession of politics and shamed the name of Canada.

I wish I could add to this accusation the further allegation that your policies have also wrought great damage to Canada, to the Liberal

1

Party, and to the profession of politics. I cannot say that, for the simple reason that you have seldom proclaimed or articulated any coherent policies. Your premiership has, for ten years, been an *ad hoc* premiership. The policies of the Liberal Party have been set forth in your vaunted Red Book. And the policies proclaimed there, in print, for all Canadians to see, you have ignored, repudiated or betrayed. Let us get down to brass tacks, shall we, Jean–Joseph?

Your Red Book announced – and solemn published announcements are taken by the public on trust, as promises to fulfil the policies set forth therein – that, among other things, you were pledged to repeal the Goods and Services Tax. This tax, made law by the previous government, you saw as a source of vast revenues. So you had no qualms in ignoring your promise, and in retaining the tax. Did you go to Parliament or to the people of Canada and explain your change of mind? No, you ignored them, and no doubt hoped the matter would be forgotten. But it was not forgotten, was it? It is still a very hot issue.

You would no doubt wish to expunge from the record books, if you could, the televised town hall meeting that took place at the CBC studio in Ottawa on December 10, 1996. The meeting was chaired by Peter Mansbridge, the CBC news anchor. A young waitress stood up–a mere slip of a 17-year old girl called Johanne Savoie–and challenged you to explain why you had lied when stating in the Red Book that you would repeal the hated GST (the Goods and Services Tax), or, if you had meant it then, why you repudiated it now. Do you remember that humiliating moment, Jean–Joseph? Yes! And don't you wish you could erase it! You hemmed and hawed. You equivocated, trying with stalling questions–cooked up by the wily practised politician you are–to put the young woman on the defensive by demanding when you had said that, and where, and who were the witnesses. You were clearly getting the worst of the exchange; the young woman was clearly making you look the devious politician you are, when mealy-mouthed Mansbridge cut short that fascinating and revealing televised drama. That young woman deserved to be appointed to Order of Canada for courage and public service. But she might have declined, when reviewing the list of existing members, and the political reasons for many of the appointments. Let's go over the transcript of the scene, shall we?

UNIDENTIFIED: Mr. Prime Minister, I'm Johanne Savoie, from Montreal. Recently, your government

awarded itself a very generous grade, "B+", based on your Red Book of campaign promises. Anyone who has taken a test, knows that on any test, some questions are worth more than others. When I voted for you, I voted for you–I didn't read the Red Book. I voted for you, based on your promise to repeal the GST. And you did not . CHRETIEN: Did you read the Red Book on that. It's not what we said in the Red Book. You should have read it. (Audience laughter) [Sycophants! Author.] UNIDENTIFIED: You were saying in all your speeches, that you were promising to repeal the GST. CHRETIEN: We always said that we were to harmonize the tax with the provincial government and we have done it with the Quebec and the Maritime provinces. We never say that it was to be repealed. Read the Red Book. It was written quite clearly. UNIDENTIFIED: What we heard during the campaign, for those of us who didn't read the Red Book and that's most of us, was that the GST was going to be repealed. CHRETIEN: No, no–we said that we were to harmonize the taxes to have a better system, because of the duplication that existed, tried to make it more simpler; but we never said in the Red Book, or directly, that it was to be scrapped. UNIDENTIFIED: I didn't hear simpler–I heard scrapped. CHRETIEN: From whom? UNIDENTIFIED: From you on television and on the radio. CHRETIEN: When?
UNIDENTIFIED: During the campaign. This is what I heard. MANSBRIDGE: Stay with us; our combined CBC/Radio Canada Town Hall with the Prime Minister, continues in a moment.

It is clear beyond any doubt that you were evading the issue by refusing to answer the direct questions put to you, by turning questions back to your interrogator, by pleading with Mansbridge to end the interview.

Mansbridge wrote about it, you remember, in *MACLEAN'S* (December 23, 2002). This is what he wrote: "the man from Shawinigan looked pretty good doing it for a couple of years – until a waitress got up one year and wanted to know why he broke his promise on scrapping the GST. That was Jean CHRÉTIEN's last town hall – even though he turned to me moments after it was over and told me he'd really enjoyed it...What he didn't enjoy was the pasting he took in the media and from inside his own party after the broadcast aired."

Of course, it is clear that you lied when you told Mansbridge that you had enjoyed it – you were terrified by the exposure of your broken promise; and Mansbridge showed himself as the mealy–mouth he was when he shut down the town hall.

But that is not the only promise you made and betrayed, is it, Jean–Joseph? I accuse you of breaking your solemn promise to appoint an Ethics Counsellor who would report to Parliament. Oh, yes, you appointed an Ethics Counsellor all right – one of your usual Liberal lackeys. But you made sure that he reported, not to Parliament, as would have been proper, but to you personally, as Prime Minister, so that you could decide unilaterally whether to accept or reject, whether to keep secret or make public, any report submitted to you on ethical matters. Why, it is almost hilarious, that an Ethics Counsellor should report to you, the minister who was to prove himself the most corrupt in the whole apparatus of government! It would be safer to entrust your comrade Mugabe with the protection of the white farmers in Zimbabwe, or your pal Castro with promoting human rights in Cuba.

That is not the end of the story of the Ethics Counsellor, is it, Jean–Joseph? Do you remember the day in Parliament, just last year, when the Opposition tabled a motion requiring that the Ethics Counsellor report in future to Parliament? The wording of the motion was copied word for word from your Red Book of promises and pledges. And you, and all your spineless, lickspittle Liberals, voted against it!! I think we will see pretzels straighten themselves out of shame before I see you or a Liberal demonstrate any familiarity with truth, scruple and honesty.

But we are getting a bit ahead of ourselves. Every informed Canadian remembers your very first acts on becoming Prime Minister in 1993. Let us recall at least three of your acts. The first thing you did was to cancel the privatization of Toronto's Pearson International

Airport, which had been negotiated, and signed, sealed, and delivered, by your predecessor, Prime Minister Brian Mulroney. You repudiated it unilaterally, and as a result you incurred for the taxpayers of Canada an enormous penalty of several hundreds of millions of dollars. That was not enough for you. What you did next, Jean–Joseph, was to cancel a legal contract with a British-Italian consortium to supply helicopters to our Air Force. For that reneging of a contract you saddled the Canadian taxpayers with a penalty of eight hundred million dollars. And you didn't bat an eyelid. No, it wasn't your money, was it? Are you more avaricious about hoarding money for yourself? But of taxpayers' money you don't give a rap, do you? (We shall talk more about that.) Then, of course, there was the issue of Free Trade with the United States, a treaty negotiated by the government of Brian Mulroney. In the election you said you would renegotiate it. Your words are available to all Canadians to read and ponder. You pledged yourself to renegotiate the Free Trade Agreement with the United States. And what did you do when you became Prime Minister? You reneged on your pledge, that's what you did.

Let us not overlook the action you took against former Prime Minister Mulroney when you instructed your attorney general to have the Royal Canadian Mounted Police initiate an investigation into an allegation that he, Mulroney, and others associated with him, had taken bribes from the Airbus Corporation to seal a contract with Air Canada rather than with Boeing. You pursued Mulroney for eight years – and no investigation could find any evidence against him. Finally the government had to settle with a payment of two million dollars to Mulroney. Even then you did not cease your harassment of your intended prey. The 'case' went for a further two years before the RCMP gave up. Your pursuit of Mulroney, like your cancelling of his helicopter contract, and his agreement with Toronto airport, all point to a personal vendetta that is unparalleled in Canadian political history, and can be explained only by a visceral hatred both of Mulroney himself, and of the party he led. We will see in due course the role that hatred, and other corroding passions, have played in the perversion of your personality, and hence of your political acts.

What disgusts the decent and honest citizen in these acts and words of yours is, first, that you subscribed to your party platform of promises without the slightest evidence that you intended to honour them; second, that you cancelled legally binding contracts without regard to the consequences for our defences; and thirdly – and this is the worst feature of your acts – you did those things autocratically, without consulting your colleagues and without debate in Parliament.

Thus, you set the seal on your method of operation in the earliest weeks of your prime ministership, and you have not wavered one iota from that method. You established that the ministers you had appointed, and the whole caucus of Liberal Members of Parliament were, as you knew them to be – in a word, amorphous creatures without backbone or scruple who would do your bidding at the snap of a finger.

Thus you established your obsession with power.

Thus, I accuse you, Jean–Joseph CHRÉTIEN, of seeking only your own advantage, celebrity, and fortune, and of pursuing them in total disregard of the harm your obsession inflicted on others, including your closest colleagues.

In the immediate aftermath of the last federal election, in the year 2000, you had your aides put out feelers with the twofold aim of sounding out popular opinion as to your contribution to Canada, and of what you should do in the coming year or so to create a "legacy". I take it that your idea of a legacy has to do intimately with how you and your governance will be judged by Posterity. (Though, of course, you would avoid all that is implied by 'judgement'. But judgement there will assuredly be. And it will not be at all favourable.)

You have been Prime Minister for ten years. Ten years, I repeat. What have you accomplished in that time? Nothing that is in the least admirable; but a very great deal that is injurious and despicable. If a Prime Minister, in office for ten years, can achieve nothing notable, nothing that has elicited the admiration of the people, and that will attract the approbation of future historians, what do you think you can achieve in the year or ten months left to you in office? Nothing. Because you cannot change. Because you will continue in your autocratic ways–in ways, that is, that render you indifferent to the needs and challenges of Canada and Canadians today and in the immediate future.

The first so-called 'legacy' project that was launched onto the airwaves to sound out public opinion, and followed up by a poll–for you live by polls, not by policies, let alone by principles–promoted the idea of a highway. Not a new highway, oh, no! That would be costly. And you have other plans for the billions collected in taxes each year. Only a refurbished highway. In fact, the old Trans-Canada Highway modernized into a divided double-lane highway from coast to coast. What a legacy! What a monument to leave behind you! The CHRÉTIEN Highway! Perhaps it occurred to you that this conception carried within it two grave flaws. First, it would be neglected and allowed to deteriorate, just as the original highway has been allowed to crumble along great stretches of it, because the Federal Government, having initiated the enterprise and funded it to the amount of 50%, then withdrew funding for its maintenance. Second, the public would, and did, see in it a source of bottomless patronage, which would allow contracts to be awarded to construction companies on the understanding that they donated sizeable contributions to the Liberal Party of Canada, in keeping with your practices of the past ten years. It was predictable, and it was predicted, that this lead balloon never left the ground; it trundled along a side street for a few yards before being abandoned in a dark back alley, where most of your advisers have their abode.

On assuming office ten years ago you concentrated all your efforts to the task of creating a Prime Minister's Office (PMO). This organism you inherited from your Liberal predecessor; who was Pierre Trudeau. His intent, and your intent, which you extended and, in a word, 'perfected', was to concentrate as much power into your own hands as possible. You anointed yourself the Richelieu of Canada. And like your model, you put statecraft before principle, and power before Christian ethics. Ah, you will protest. What do Christian ethics have to do with politics? Obviously you, Jean–Joseph, a self–proclaimed Roman Catholic, choose not to heed the Pope. We will consider this issue later.

Your PMO numbers no fewer than 105 people, headed by a Chief of Staff in whom you have invested enormous powers which you have wrested unconstitutionally from Ministers of the Crown.[1] Therein lies your especial victory. That

---

[1] 1 It is worth noting that throughout the Second World War, Winston Churchill, the Prime Minister of Great Britain, had a personal staff of all of five people. But, in character with a true democracy, even of a democracy at war, Churchill knew he had to persuade his colleagues, not dictate to them. For he knew that, in a democracy, ministers of the Crown will not be dictated to.

victory lies in the perversion of a system of government that is one of the chiefest virtues of a free and democratic society. In a word, your have bent all your efforts to undermining the foundations of democratic and responsible government in Canada. How have you done this? Your main instrument has been, for appointment to offices of the Crown, the selection of men and women who you judged to be ambitious and venal. It is well established that corrupt men have an insight into the weaknesses of others. Your selection was unerring. You picked–with a few exceptions--incompetent and fawning people who put their positions and their 'perks' ahead of the interests of the country, and who swallowed the only 'principle' you ever enunciated, namely, loyalty to the Liberal Party of Canada, above all other loyalties and principles. It was, of course, understood, that this loyalty was 'sworn' to the Leader of the Party, rather than to the Party itself. As to country, forget it. And as to oaths of office, solemnly sworn to on the Bible, you and the sycophants you have selected as ministers of the Crown, well, they are so much hot air, not to be taken seriously. 'Solemnly' doesn't enter into it. The fitting word is: 'blasphemously'.

You want concrete examples? It is common knowledge–for you and others involved have openly boasted about it–that you pour public moneys into ridings that have returned Liberal MPs to Ottawa; and when other constituencies complain that they are starved of government funding for worthwhile projects, you sneer at them and spout the Liberal mantra: "If you want government moneys for your projects, you had better return a Liberal MP and he or she will work for you and you will get results." That Liberal policy–or rather, your personal agenda–is called Corruption. It is nothing less than a form of bribery. Of bribery, furthermore, with public funds. Do you know what corruption is? Of course you do. For every day you and your colleagues work like beavers, gnawing away at the pillars that sustain the structure of rightful government, while trying to present this improper use of public funds as a perfectly normal practice of government. And talking about MPs' constituencies, let's talk about yours. You have always claimed that when you direct public funds to projects in your constituency you are only carrying out your normal duties as a Member of Parliament. But you are not just a member of Parliament: you are the Prime Minister. That position carries with it a responsibility for transparent and above the board conduct which you have proven yourself morally incapable of grasping, or politically unwilling to live up to. As an MP you are beholden solely to your electors. A prime minister acts in the service of all Canadians. It is difficult to put the finger on any single act of yours that was meant to be carried out for all Canadians The extent of your venality becomes clear when it is known that you have personally ordered the pouring of more public funds into your own small Quebec constituency of Shawinigan in the past five years than have been allocated for public works to the whole Province of Alberta. That level of corruption merits the charge of villainy. That villainy comprises both a manifest bigotry and hostility to Alberta, and a level of bribery and chauvinism that has never been seen before in Canada.

You have bought the loyalty of Liberal MPs by appointing as many as possible to State departments as Ministers of the Crown and as Deputy Ministers. You have no fewer than 39 government departments, headed by ministers who 'rule' over bureaucracies, some vast, others pettifogging, who themselves issue regulations and edicts, generally without the approval of the ministers, because they know that the ministers, despite their oaths of office, seldom make decisions in the areas of public policy.

They have to get the approval of the Prime Minister's Office for any important decision that has to be made, whenever you are out of your office, or out of the country, which is much of the time. Thirty–nine departments of State! And the United States federal government numbers only nine! What do those people do for their money? And then, of course, if one of them blunders so flagrantly that information about his or her incompetence or venality cannot be hidden from a prying press, you quickly promote them. That is, you quickly move them to a remote position, or you sideline them briefly, only to be restored to favour when the scandal has died down. That is what you did in the infamous Gagliano case.

Alfonso Gagliano, you will remember, was the minister of Corporate Development, and your personal minister for Quebec affairs. When his approved conduct was exposed – he was giving out lucrative contracts to Quebec companies, without public tenders, with the sure confidence that those companies would make substantial donations to the Liberal Party – although he was only following your example and encouragement, you did not sack him, still less charge him with corrupt practices. Oh, no! For that would be tantamount to laying yourself open to indictment. What you did was to promote him. And at the same time you got rid of him by sending him out of the country as ambassador to Denmark, so that he could not be interrogated. Thus, at a stroke, you approved corruption, you rewarded corruption, and you undermined the careers, and indeed the very principle underlying the profession of the foreign service. That operation is called, by some: 'You scratch my back and I'll scratch yours.' You, of course, give it the exalted name of 'Party Loyalty'. Honest people call it either, 'Birds of a feather', or, more fittingly, 'Thick as thieves.'

Think of it: 39 government departments. I will wager that not one Canadian in 100,000 can name all of them. I will wager furthermore that not one of your own Liberal MPs can name them all! As for the people who head those departments, it is even less likely that your own Party members have the any idea who they are. There are three reasons for that: one, they are too numerous; two, many of them are unimportant; and three, they get changed around so often.

Let us review the departments of State whose heads, that is, ministers, pay homage and subservience to you. Here they are, most of them at least, drawn up in the list provided by

the Department of the Secretary of State
responsible for the Civil Service:

- ☿ Transport
- ☿ Environment
- ☿ Public Works
- ☿ Fisheries and Oceans
- ☿ Canadian Heritage
- ☿ Finance
- ☿ Industry
- ☿ Justice
- ☿ Human Resources Development
- ☿ Intergovernmental Affairs
- ☿ Labour
- ☿ Health
- ☿ Agriculture
- ☿ International Trade
- ☿ Natural Resources
- ☿ Indian Affairs
- ☿ Citizenship and Immigration
- ☿ Veterans Affairs
- ☿ International Corporations
- ☿ National Defence
- ☿ Solicitor General
- ☿ Children and Youth
- ☿ Multiculturalism
- ☿ International Trade.
- ☿ Asia–Pacific
- ☿ Federal Economic Development
- ☿ Initiative for Northern Ontario, and Rural Development

- International Financial Institutions
- Amateur Sport
- Foreign Affairs
- Central & East European & Middle East
- Latin America and Africa
- Francophonie
- Western Economic Diversification

As the reader's eye runs down this list, he may wonder: How is it that the affairs of State are ranged in that order? Do you know? It is most assuredly the question that will rise to the surface of a host of questions prompted by this list. This list, I repeat, is the official list provided by the Canadian government. Does it reflect the relative importance of the portfolios according to your personal prejudices and interests? Does it suggest that the ministers and secretaries responsible for these portfolios come from the most politically sensitive constituencies? Is it, in fact, just a random list without any particular significance? Whatever the answer, whatever the explanation, the list by itself constitutes a scathing indictment of your government, and hence of yourself. For government, which necessarily occupies itself with a large range of responsibilities, must order them according to a hierarchy of importance in terms of national security and the national interest.

The answer to the question will probably not occur to anyone. It is this: the departments of State are listed according to the seniority in Cabinet of the ministers who occupy them. That explains why the most important of the offices of State, namely, foreign affairs, defence, and internal security are invisible. In the mere ten years of your régime, you have had no fewer than four ministers of Foreign Affairs; five ministers of International Trade, five ministers of Defence, and four Solicitors–General (responsible for the Royal Canadian Mounted Police and the Canadian Security & Intelligence Service, and hence for internal security). We note, incidentally, that Citizenship and Immigration, which is of paramount importance in matters of internal security and social unity, is also way down the list.

The next question is a corollary to the first: Why would you, as prime minister, switch your ministers about so frequently? After all, what can they learn about their jobs in two or three years? What, indeed! And why indeed! That is precisely your plan. I accuse you, Jean–Joseph, of deliberately removing and bringing in new ministers precisely in order that they should not learn their portfolios. If they were there long enough they might just learn

how   to   master   their   departmental
responsibilities and bureaucracies. You could
never tolerate that. You can handle the civil
servants, all right. After all, most come from
Quebec, and most owe their positions to you.
They know who they serve, don't they, when it
comes to pensions and voting time?

What about the portfolios listed first
then? It seems fairly obvious that if they had
occupied those portfolios longer than any other
ministers,   it   must   be   because   they   had
mastered their portfolios and had become the
most competent in their jobs. Let's look at them,
shall we? They are: Transport, Environment,
Fisheries and Oceans, and Canadian Heritage.
These areas of national policy are clearly not of
the first importance. Who are the ministers in
charge? Why, they're our old friends Collenette,
Anderson, Thibault, and Sheila Copps. Are
these people competent? Four more loyal
Liberals, four more intellectually challenged
people, would be hard to find among the serried
ranks of Liberal members to choose from. Of
course, that is precisely why you appointed
them. As for them, with the next administration
they will be gone like a puff of dandelion seed. (I
was wrong on one.) For them now, the celebrity
and the perks of the moment are all that
counts. Let us see what they have accomplished
during their many years in the same office.

TRANSPORT

When we Canadians say "Transport" we think first of all of the air and the ground; that is, of airlines and both railways and the highways, all of which traverse this huge country of ours. Yet we hear little, from day to day and from week to week, either in our private newspapers or on our public broadcast stations, of our national means of transportation, unless it is bad news. Do we ever hear from David Collenette, explaining what his national policies are in respect of our airlines, our railways, and our highways?

But of course, you rarely let your Cabinet colleagues pronounce on policy, do you? So tell me, what are your policies in these fields of transportation? You have none. No, that is not entirely true. You announce a policy on your government web site. Here is your statement:

> Transportation is essential to our well-being. Canadians need a reliable, safe and sustainable transportation system to connect our communities, and to connect us with our trading partners Transport Canada works to help ensure that Canadians have the best transportation system by developing and administering policies, regulations and programs for a safe, efficient and environmentally friendly transportation system; contributing to Canada's

economic growth and social development; and, protecting the physical environment.

If that statement is the best that you can do by way of enunciating a "policy", it is at least consistent with nearly everything you and your government do and say–namely, it says nothing, and is a piece of flim–flam concealing insincerity and duplicity. I will have more to say about it when we come to environmental issues. For the time being, let us look at some of your achievements in the realm of transport.

Rail. How is it that the trains get derailed so frequently on our national tracks? The answer is obvious: because you know nothing about railways, and you care less. Hence you slap down any minister who seeks, responsibly, to spend the money necessary to maintain the tracks in a safe condition. So they become degraded. And the frequent derailments not only cost lives; they also cause the spilling of highly toxic substances which poison earth, air and water; and disrupt people's lives by the enforced evacuation of their homes. I do not recall ever having heard you show that you cared anything for those people, or for the condition of our railroads.

Canada is a vast country. Its size alone calls aloud for a high-speed coast-to-coast passenger rail service, on the model of Europe's. Think of the tourism potential alone! It is said that Canadian engineers invented the continuous welded track that permits the very high-speed trains of today. But we don't have any. Why not? Why have you never taken the slightest interest in the railways of Canada? Because your mind is elsewhere. (I will analyse later the contents of your mind–and the picture I have to present is not a nice one.) It is said that because of the great difference between the summer and winter temperatures in Canada, especially in the Prairies, a continuous welded track is not possible. But I have heard it rumoured that Canadian engineers have overcome this difficulty. But you are not in the slightest bit interested. Why? Because such a rail system would redo what MacDonald's railway did in 1887–that is, go a bit of the way to reuniting the country in a time of division. And, despite your pious utterances, that is the last thing you want. That statement will surprise many people. It will not surprise you. But it will alarm you, for it will make you realize that someone has finally penetrated your mask and caught a glimpse of your secret agenda.

Air. Your bungling, indecision and favouritism have destroyed competitive air travel, and resulted in one national airline. We are finally seeing that Air Canada is a financial disaster, whereas one small independent regional airline is a roaring success. You are driven by a one-track mind that thrives on autocracy and étatisme, and is terrified of genuine competition. Our one national and international airline will only be stirred into action by opening up our air routes to foreign competition. Perhaps it is too late.

Highways. We have already said a word about our highways, and how the federal government, having initiated the building of the trans–Canada highway and paid for 50% of its costs, has steadily reduced its share of the maintenance of the highway. Not only that, but it is not even completed: for long stretches, being still only a single lane highway. When you consider that the population of Canada and its major routes of communication are restricted to a band measuring only about 300 miles wide north of the Canada/US border, and compare that with the vast area of the United States, and then compare their highways with ours, one can only wonder about your national priorities and where the billions of dollars collected in taxes are spent every year. On the question of highways, however, there is another factor. You yourself have promoted an international anti–pollution treaty. You and those of your persuasion claim that the burning of fossil fuels is one of the worst culprits in the spewing of poisons into the air, injurious to our health and causing global warming. If you believed that, you would bend your energies to the transport of most of the goods that cross our country and that are imported from and exported to the United States–after all, 85% of our external trade is with the United States–by rail, and not by trucks. But you don't, do you? Why not?

When we talk roads and highways we think inescapably of the toll in deaths, injuries, bereavements, and other forms of suffering, quite apart from the sheer physical destruction and economic damage. Do you know how many people are killed each year on our roads and highways? The figure is a staggering five thousand. You could do something about that. What's that you say? Highways and roads are not a federal responsibility? Nor is health, under the Constitution, but you made sure it became your business.. (Responsibility, that is another thing; and we will come to that.) You could do something about the awful carnage, by your mere influence, if you put your mind to it. But you do nothing. Why? Because you don't care.

Shipping. Canada has the longest coastline of any country in the world. Yet we are virtually

devoid of anything that can be called a serious
fleet of ships. I will talk later about defence and
security. But, for the moment, what do you say
to the idea of a cruise line specializing in
Round–Canada Arctic cruises? Do we have a
cruise line? No. Why not? Canada used to have
a fleet of great trans–Atlantic liners. Today?
Nothing. True, the age of the great
trans–Atlantic liners is over, displaced by
airliners. But our huge coastline is still there,
beckoning for Canadian shipping to explore our
maritime treasures. You are not interested? You
have other weighty concerns of State to occupy
your time? Yes, and other enterprises,
vote-buying enterprises, to lavish public funds
on!

But wait a moment! I seem to recall that
the former Minister of Finance–what's his name,
now? Oh, yes, Paul Martin–he has a huge fleet
of ships. His company is called the Canadian
Steamship Lines. But his ships are all engaged
in global freight, aren't they? Moreover, they are
all registered off–shore, in so–called third world
countries like Honduras, in order to evade both
the taxes they would have to pay if registered in
Canada, and the safety inspections which they
now get away with, and the fair wages for a fair
day's work.

Canada, to repeat, once had a great fleet of liners. Today, nothing. We should have a fleet of cruise liners. The cruise business has never been so popular and profitable. Our waters are among the most popular on Earth. And we have nothing. Such an enterprise requires imaginative and creative initiatives on the part of both business and government. Business to create, and government to encourage and smooth the path. Yet, nothing. Why not? It is probably, in part at least, because business wealth is concentrated in Ontario and Quebec, and the officials and people of those provinces are land-locked in their mentality. If they look beyond the bounds of their own territories, they look either to Ottawa, for help, or they look south, to the United States. The same is true, in spades, of the bureaucrats of Ottawa and Toronto: they are inward looking, visionless, pension-seeking, security-craving, novelty-suffocating, regulation-bound, routine-minded committee-men.

Open your eyes, man! You haven't travelled much in this great country of ours, except for political grandstanding and photo-ops. Not to look and learn. You know nothing west of Ottawa. I will explain why later. But look at a map. Just look at the vast spaces of those regions of Western Canada that we call

The Prairies. Look closer. What do you see? Yes,
I know what you see, what goes on in your
mind: you see resources to be exploited, wealth
to be taxed. You fail to see the vast systems of
lakes and rivers. A man of vision, a statesman,
would look at those waterways and be inspired
to create a number of consortiums and charge
them with the bold enterprise of developing
them and opening them up for every imaginable
kind of craft, for navigation from the rivers and
lakes in the south as far as the Arctic Ocean.
We would see hundreds of resort lodges spring
up all over Canada. Not only would they attract
Canadians in their tens of thousands, intent on
exploring their own country; they would be a
magnet for millions of adventure-hungry
Europeans, who are drawn to Canada largely for
our wildlife. Oh, for another man of vision!
What's that you say? – mosquitoes, black flies,
bulldogs, no-seeums? Of course, how silly of
me! I was forgetting. We must let the
environmentalists get their way! After all,
mosquitoes have the right to live too. (The bats,
swallows and dragonflies have their rights
too-to eat mosquitoes! Now if we humans could
come up with a tasty mosquito-quiche, it would
be all right. But just kill them? Never! I figure
that the people of the Po Valley must be
eternally grateful there were no tree-huggers

and bug–lovers in Italy when they eliminated malaria in the 19th century.)

ENVIRONMENT

Ah, the environment! Now there's a portfolio you can get your teeth into! Custom–made for an international grandstander of your calibre! The environment is a hot international topic, sponsored, promoted, financed and publicized by dozens of organizations, global, national, regional and local. Not only does it give you a rare chance to appear to be genuinely interested in doing good: it also offers a heaven–sent opportunity to carry favour with the people involved in the environmental movement and their uninformed fellow-travellers, and to exploit a great source of votes – all for the small price of handing out a few millions a year to those organizations.

Your spokesman in this enterprise, the minister for the Environment, David Anderson – or your spokesman on the few occasions when you are not occupying centre stage – has followed your lead in the matter like the loyal lap dog he is. Of course, the big event in Canada environmentally is the Kyoto Accord. I am sure you will agree that there is no need to go into the goals and provisions of this international agreement, beyond reminding readers that it seeks to reduce the volume of carbohydrates being poured into the atmosphere by the burning of fossil fuels. The theory is that the Earth is passing through a stage characterized by the warming of the atmosphere, and that this potentially dangerous warming is caused directly by man and his industrial activities.

There are two major problems with this Accord, and the theory. The first is that the nations which cause the most pollution of the atmosphere–China, Russia, India, and Brazil–are exempted from the Accord. And secondly, there is only connnflicting scientific evidence to support the contention that the Earth is warming, or that, if there is any warming, it is caused by man's activities.

Of course, you won't be deterred by these objections. You won't bother to wait for science to reach a firmer conclusion. You will bulldoze ahead, simply because it looks good. You don't really care whether the theory has merit or not. For once, you will be seen on the 'right' side of a controversial issue of international ramifications. And what a legacy to leave behind! Yes, indeed – what a legacy to leave to your successors, after you retire in February 2004. You have ratified the Accord, without having drawn up any plans detailing how the Accord is to be implemented, and without having calculated any of the costs that are certain to be entailed in lost production, lost corporate returns on their investments, and lost employment. Worse by far, you crashed ahead with the ratification of the Accord in the teeth of wholesale opposition from the Provinces. I suppose that, in your view, it is sufficient sometimes to appear to be on the side of good, and to hell with reality.

I save for the last the most important accusation I can level at you. It is simply this – and it is the ploy that all devious politicians resort to. You put the burden of sacrifice for meeting the obligations you have unilaterally undertaken onto others, while evading them yourself. Don't try to worm your way out of it: it's the truth. You have laid it on the provinces, on corporations, and on the mass of individual Canadians to use less energy of all kinds, while you in government continue in your profligate ways. I could mention a hundred instances, but I will mention two. They may seem small potatoes, but they add up to mountains of waste. First, there's the matter of postage stamps. You permit the packaging of five stamps in a folder that is many times the weight and worth of the stamps themselves. Multiply those folders by millions, and see not only how many trees they represent, but how much energy is needed to produce the folders. Secondly, you and your thousands of ministers, MPs and civil servants travel all over Canada and the world at public expense, by air and by car, often enough on unnecessary junkets, and by the consumption of millions of barrels of oil you contribute more to the pollution of the atmosphere than ten times that number of ordinary citizens. Have you issued a decree limiting travel by those people? Of course not!

Have you cut back on your own lavish and wasteful travelling? Of course not! Why ask you, the prime minister, to set an example! No, sirree! That's not leadership, is it? And to think that you bought two super deluxe airliners at a cost of one hundred million dollars from the Quebec company which you have subsidized more lavishly than any other company in Canada, for the sole task of transporting you and your favoured cronies about the world. I repeat: one hundred million dollars, while you deny the slimmest of pensions to the widows of our Armed Forces veterans. Villain is too mild a word for you.

FISHERIES AND OCEANS

Who speaks on behalf of all Canada in this key department? What does he have to say? Who allowed the extermination of the cod fishery off the shores of Newfoundland? And who came within an ace of doing the same thing with the Pacific salmon on the West Coast? I'll tell you who. It was civil servants 'advising' your ministers, three thousand miles from the scenes, under your 'leadership', for the reason that cod and salmon don't pull in big bucks or big votes.–While we're on the subject of fisheries and oceans, let's talk for a minute about our lakes and rivers. Did you know that Canada has greater resources in lakes and rivers than any other country in the world? Of course you didn't. Why don't you? Because you couldn't care about Canada–especially about Western Canada, where most of the rivers and lakes are. Canada is a great attraction to foreign visitors. Can you imagine what an attraction our lakes and rivers could be, both for holiday cruising and fishing, no matter how remote–indeed, the remoter the better–if properly exploited and publicized? Of course you don't! And why not? Because your mind is preoccupied with two or three obsessions at the most. (I will develop this fascinating topic later.)

AGRICULTURE

What is being done for our farmers in the face of the massive subsidies paid out by the American and European governments to their farmers? And who is doing it? No one knows. And what does the press have to say about it? If the grain in question had been Quebec grain, the response from Ottawa would have been different to the tune of several billions of dollars.–Why do you persist in the federal fraud that is the Canadian Wheat Board, which robs Western grain farmers of millions of dollars every year? For one reason only: that it is Western grain. You know perfectly well that no 'wheat board' would ever be tolerated in Quebec, and that the Liberal government would never dare inflict a wheat board on Quebec. Why, there is not even a wheat board in Ontario either. And since we are talking about Quebec, why is it that they enjoy a monopoly on dairy products, permitting them to export their wares, and to ban the import of similar products from outside? On that subject, we might as well ask why it is that, although Canada has a Free Trade Agreement with the United States and Mexico, binding on the Provinces, there is no free trade between the Provinces. Why? For the simple reason that it is in Quebec's interest to erect trade barriers if they are to her advantage.

This policy is, of course, the work of Quebec people in Ottawa.

LUMBER EXPORTS

Same thing here. Most of the softwood lumber exports to the United States are from British Columbia and Alberta, provinces which can be dismissed. The softwood lumber exporters of Quebec have already been bought off by secret funds. If the United States can unilaterally impose prohibitive duties on Canadian softwood imports, for the sole reason that the protection of domestic softwood in certain states will favour the re-election of Republican politicians, and our government under your 'leadership' does nothing, out of sheer cowardice, there is no hope whatever of your retaliating by reducing our exports to the U.S. of oil and gas and electricity, without which their houses and industries would be shut down overnight. It is bad enough having to put up with you as a corrupt prime minister. It is even worse having you as a spineless prime minister.

IMMIGRATION

When we think of Immigration we think automatically of Eleanor Caplan. And when we think of Eleanor Caplan–or even worse, envisage her–we cannot but recall to mind the fat British erstwhile Labour MP, Bessie Braddock, and the sharp exchange which took place between her and Winston Churchill in the House of Commons these many years ago.

It appears that Churchill mentioned Bessie's being fat and ugly. Whereupon Bessie accused Winston of being drunk. To which Winston replied that he would be sober in the morning. The main difference between Bessie Braddock and Eleanor Caplan is that Bessie was also very bright. Your former Minister of Immigration was, and is, not only fat and ugly, but also stupid. But then, it is well established that you choose stupid and/or docile people to be ministers of the Crown, for the simple reason that you yourself, being intellectually challenged, can then comfortably lord it over them.

You got rid of Fat Caplan two years ago because of a foul-up in her department. It involved the unholy stink of bribes in our Canadian High Commission in Hong Kong, which employed local (unvetted) people to vet applicants for refugee or immigrant status. You may have known about it. If you did, you permitted it, because you know that the great majority of Asian immigrants and refugees find their way to the Western Provinces, where they will swell the increasing numbers of residents, small though they are today, who will be encouraged to vote for the Liberal party in future elections. Again, if you knew of it, there is no evidence that you took any steps to find out whether similar practices are carried on in any of our Embassies and High Commissions. If you did not know about this corrupt practice, we must infer, either that our Foreign Service knew nothing about it, or that, knowing, they did not bother to tell you.

Who is the minister for immigration today? Some fellow called Coderre. Who has ever heard any public statement from him, or from any previous any minister of immigration in the past ten years? For that matter, what national newspaper or radio or television station has ever, *has ever*, interviewed any immigration minister in the past ten years with the view to fulfilling its public function, that is, of informing Canadians what the Government's policy is, or is not? – and of comparing such statements with what the Government is, and is not doing, in the field of immigration?

But we know well enough what your policy is, secret though it is, for the effects of your secret agenda are visible for all to see. Your immigration policy, like your refugee policy, is dictated by your slavish pursuit of, and control by, 'political correctness.' This ideology favours anyone other than people of white European birth and culture. (Except, be it noted, those who speak French and are destined for Quebec, to which province you have abdicated your responsibilities.) Not only that: the moment any refugee or illegal immigrant arrives on these shores, you provide them with free hotels and meals, and free legal services. More, you pay for them to take lessons in the language of their choice, despite the fact that they have already arrived in a country ready to immerse themselves in this new linguistic culture. All of these services are provided out of public funds, far in excess of any funds available to our own people who may have fallen on hard times and in need of temporary welfare assistance. But you have made a calculation, haven't you? You have had your obedient Liberal–voting civil servants calculate that there are far more immigrants each year than destitute Canadians.

NOTICE TO ALL IMMIGRANTS AND REFUGEES (legal & illegal)

You may believe that you are coming to a free country. That is not correct. If you are granted a visa or other entry, you will be restricted in various ways. Illegal refugees will be provided with free hotel accommodation, free meals, free medical services, and free legal advice. However, you will not be required to stay in your hotels, and if you leave without giving an address where you may be contacted, you may be assured that the authorities will not search for you. This ruling also applies to known or suspected terrorists.

Refugees who have been declared legal will be released immediately following their vetting. They will be provided with the names of lawyers, paid by the government, who will take up their causes, if any. Immigrants from the poorest countries of Africa and Asia will be given priority over others. (In fact, most Europeans need not apply. This refers particularly to English-speaking people.) Applicants from Asia and Africa need not submit a police record, or a medical record.

If you speak French you may prefer to settle in Quebec. If you do so, you will find out soon enough that discrimination exists against English-speaking citizens. Of course, it is not really discrimination: the laws and customs are merely in force to protect the integrity of the Québec language, which is threatened by the dominance of English. If you speak real French, you may have some difficulty in understanding

Québec French, but you are encouraged to persist until you learn to speak correctly. If, on the other hand, you hear speakers on radio and television who speak real French, do not be discouraged; and above all do not try to emulate them. We are working on them as much as we can.

If you come from a disadvantaged country of Africa or Asia, and if you settle in any province west of Quebec, you will find yourself among the minority races. The Government of Canada is doing its best -- indeed, they are working day and night, year in and year out -- to level the playing field so that you will find the ground tilted in your favour. That means that, if you hear any derogatory remark made by a white person -- or even if you make one up -- you should lay a complaint immediately against the white person with the Human Rights Commission, and they will spare no effort in persecuting -- er, prosecuting -- the person or persons accused. On the other hand, since the white people are in the majority, and since they hold most of the economic cards, you may slander and libel them as much as you please without fear of recrimination. At least, the authorities will not help them. However, you should be warned that they might sue you in civil court. This is unlikely, since litigation will likely incur lawyers' expenses of many thousands of dollars; and the verdict is likely to go against the plaintiffs. We should know, because the Prime Minister has appointed all the judges. Ha, ha, ha!

You should be aware that certain restrictions on your freedoms are in force. For example, if you find work, which is not assured, you will probably have to join a trades union and pay union dues. Even if you don't join, you will still have to pay union dues. This is because if we made union membership a matter of choice, union members would never vote for us. Similarly, our greatly famous and renowned Charter of Rights and Freedoms does not assure the right to private property. The reasons for that restriction are so obvious that it is not necessary to spell them out.

Finally, the government is exploring all the ways it can exploit to restrict and limit Canadian citizens' freedom of speech and expression, in the belief that criticism of government and its agencies is likely to cause dissension and social disunity, and in the conviction that in all matters of public policy -- social, economic, cultural and other -- Government knows best what is good and right for its citizens.

CANADIAN HERITAGE

The minister who is in charge of the department which fosters and promotes what it is pleased to call the Canadian Heritage is the MP for Hamilton, one Sheila Copps.

I like Mrs Copps. She is not only an attractive young woman, she is also refreshingly outgoing and outspoken, and the sole bright spark in a government that exudes deceit, denial and duplicity. Indeed, the observer must wonder sometimes why a woman such as Sheila Copps would ever associate herself with such enemies of the people as you and your thousands of other colleagues and associates.

That she is a fervently proud Canadian cannot be questioned. She really seems to believe everything she says, when she talks about Canada. (Which is the very opposite of what we can say about you, Jean–Joseph.) Yes, even when she talks utter rubbish, which is most of the time, our patriotic Sheila really believes it.

Yes, Sheila is a refreshing adjunct to the gang you have assembled around you in Ottawa. If I were a prisoner in solitary, and fed on a diet of anaemic Liberal cabbage soup every day, Sheila would come across like a succulent worm in this gruel.

Do you remember the day, not far distant in the past, like three years, when some guy screamed a 'song' in a Molson's TV commercial? It was immediately called "the Canadian rant". Sheila went bananas! She was so fired up with Canadian patriotism and enraptured by the power of Canadian beer and the commercial message that she had three hundred thousand little Canadian flags made and sent them out to all the schools in Canada. My, what fervour! What great national feeling! What devotion to duty! (The fact that the singer left for the United States the next day to make a better living does not sully our beautiful and abiding picture of him as a true patriot.)

Heritage, Culture, Tradition. Beautiful words! Even more beautiful concepts and values. And we know that you and all your colleagues are the greatest champions of "Canadian values". You have even, now and again, favoured us with your notion of them. You know - things like compassion, caring, tolerance, non-discrimination, and even multiculturalism, bilingualism and political correctness. That is the stuff of which to build your great legacy! And Sheila Copps is your worthy standard–bearer. Let's ask her what she understands by Heritage, Culture, Tradition, shall we?

Sheila: Heritage? That's easy. Heritage is all that we value from the past and is of value and relevance today in the lives of Canadians.

Question: Such as?

Sheila: Well, such as, er, well, such as, er, what about the tepee?

Question: And Tradition?

Sheila : That's easy. Tradition is all that's most valuable in our past history and is still revered today.

Question: Such as?

Sheila: Well, such as, er, well, such as, er – what about the Riel Rebellion?

Question: And Culture?

Sheila: Well, such as, er, well such as, er – well, as you know as well as I, Culture plays an immensely important role in the lives of all Canadians. Why, without Culture, we wouldn't be Canadians, now would we? Where would we, as Canadians be, without Culture? Culture is our very lifeblood. It gives meaning and direction to all our lives as Canadians. Now doesn't it? Eh? I mean, Culture in Canada is a huge industry. Like steel and basketball and peaches, it brings in millions of dollars a year in much needed revenue to the Government of Canada. Eh?

Question: Can you sum them all up in one supreme example, Minister?

Sheila: Sure! I can sum them all up in one supreme example. Now and again, in the course of an excavation to build a shopping mall or an apartment block, someone digs up a bone. The news gets out. An aboriginal leader descends on the site and proclaims it "Sacred land!" He is right! I take his side. It is the Canadian thing to do. Canadian values are at stake. Canadian tradition is in the balance. Canadian culture is alive and vibrant!

I might ask Sheila a question like this:

"Tell me, Sheila, which of the Group of Seven do you consider the best of all?"

"Well, it's got to be the United States. After all, they're the most powerful."

"No, I mean, the Group of Seven painters. You know, the Canadian painters."

"Oh, why didn't you say so! That's easy. Since they're all Canadians, they're all equal."

To Sheila, culture means only what it means to anthropologists. To a European, or a Chinese, or a South American, it is different. There is more culture in the poorest of Mexican villages than in the whole of Sheila's constituency.

INDIAN AFFAIRS

Let's skip over Industry, Justice, Human Resources, and Intergovernmental Affairs – except as we treat of them incidentally – and go straight to what you call Indian Affairs. You were once the Minister for Indian Affairs, weren't you? Yes, you were – for a period of about five years. What did you do for them? Nothing Oh, except for one thing: you poured money into them, as you continue, as Prime Minister, to pour money into them. But, I repeat: What have you done for them? Worse than nothing, for they are in far greater distress today than they were ten years ago, when you

became Prime Minister. Let's go on a visit to a
typical Indian Reservation, shall we? Yes, come
on. I know you're reluctant; and we all know the
motive behind your reluctance. But I am going
to drag you with me, willy-nilly.

Actually, Jean–Joseph, a lot of Indian
Reservations resemble each other, don't they?
Let's go to this one. What do you see? The whole
area where they live is like a junkyard. There
are rusted cars and trucks lying all over the
place. Abandoned equipment, fairly new but
now discarded, lies here and there. Laundry,
mostly looking rather grey, hangs out on
washing lines. There are no flowerbeds, no
flowers, and not even any vegetables. Only
weeds and rank grass. A number of children
saunter around listlessly, not knowing what to
do. They are grubby and dressed in poor
clothes. The whole area has an air of
hopelessness about it: uncared for, wracked
with poverty, uneducated, despairing. In nearby
suburbs they see well cared-for houses and
gardens; but they seem to have no impact on
them. Why should they? What have they got to
care for?

Where are their leaders? Why, the
leaders of some Reservations pull in huge
payments from your Government, and live in

affluent suburbs in the nearest cities. Yes, sums like $180,000 a year, tax free, and they are as indifferent to the plight of their charges as you are.

Now let's go to an Inuit settlement, shall we? Look around you, Jean-Joseph, will you? No, you don't want to. You won't like what you see. For what you see you are responsible for. What you see is the direct result of your neglect or social engineering. You ordered the resettlement of an entire colony of relatively happy people from their ancestral lands to an unprepared cluster of huts in Newfoundland. There they had nothing to occupy them. You transplanted them, and then abandoned them. What do you see? Just look at those poor children! What on earth are they doing? Look, dammit! Look at them! They are peering into plastic bags and – no, they are putting their faces into the bags and taking deep breaths. What is in those bags? Look, now they are reeling. They have inane looks on their faces. Oh, they are falling down! They are writhing on the ground, still with those haunted expressions on their faces. My God, who has done that evil thing to those poor children?

But where are their parents? You don't know, you say? I think you do. But you prefer to sweep it under the rug,- or better, pass this human tragedy on to your underlings, and when they mismanage it, accuse them of having caused the problem in the first place. Let's ask one of these children where their parents are. Where? Oh, in those huts over there? Thank you. Can we go and see them? No? Why not? Better not? Well, we'll go any way. - Come on, Jean-Joseph, you are going to come with me even if I have to drag you by the scruff of the neck.

Oh, my God, I can't believe what I see. One glance is enough - ten or twenty men and women, together, incoherent.... I can't go on. It is too horrible.

But what is this? We go over to the next hut, where we have seen through the window a spectacle... Oh, no, I can't believe it. A boy of about 16 years is hanging from a beam....

Are you satisfied, Jean-Joseph? That is your work. Everything we have seen is your handiwork. You are personally responsible for those great human tragedies. You just don't give a damn. You have never given a damn about the plight and the suffering of your fellow-Canadians. Is that the direct consequence of "da Canadian values".

We all know another of your great "Canadian values": it is to throw vast sums of hard-earned tax moneys at problems you can't be bothered to try to resolve by honest methods and purpose. You throw hundreds of millions of dollars at them, with the intent either to bribe or to appease.

Yes, I know: the problems of our indigenous peoples are fraught with difficulties. But you have run away from them. For the past ten years – indeed for a hundred years, there has been a crying need to enshrine their rights into solemn treaties, but you have turned your back on them. You seem lacking in the most basic elements of Humanity.

But let us be quite clear about one thing. Just because our indigenous peoples have been outrageously treated in the past – and by the past I mean, for the last hundred years – that does not mean that every case involving our native peoples, whether as a class or as individuals, should be decided in their favour, out of a misplaced sympathy. Yet that is the intent of the doctrine of affirmative action. Or reverse discrimination. A state doesn't rectify one injustice by committing another. There is, right now, before the courts in Ontario, a case involving three-year old twin sisters. They have been the foster children of two loving parents for the past two years. But the sisters are of half Indian parentage. Their mother, an Indian, who was incapable of caring for them, abandoned them and they were made the wards of the State. Now that their final destiny is about to be decided, the Indian mother's band has involved itself in the dilemma and demanded that the little girls be surrendered to the band. Instead of the Provincial family court dealing with it in the obvious interest of the children, the foster parents, fearful of losing their children, have had to resort to the courts, albeit at great expense to themselves. The greatest fear of all decent people is that the court may be swayed by the false arguments of the Indian band lawyers and find in favour of so-called native cultural rights, and award the Indian band custody of the children, in the teeth of all the evidence that cries out aloud for the upholding of the fundamental rights of the children.

HEALTH

There is a Canada Health Act. You are often preaching about health. At the enactment of the Canada Health Act, your fellow-liberals vowed to finance the costs of this Act to the tune of 50%. Today, having welched on your agreements, you have progressively reduced your government's contribution to about 15% of the total, the rest being borne by the Provinces. No wonder your vaunted health system is on the rocks. And what do you do? Why, you do what you always do: you put the blame on others.

As I say, there is a Canada Health Act. It is a federal Act. Although health is within the jurisdiction of the Provinces, under our Constitution, you and your predecessors bribed the Provinces to surrender control to the Federal Government. No greater error has ever been committed by Provincial Governments.

The Canada Health Act contains five essential criteria. I won't bother to list them. Suffice it to say that they are binding on the Provinces, because the Provinces have surrendered to Ottawa their control over HEALTH in their Provinces.

The fact is that the Health Act is the biggest political trick ever inflicted on a trusting Canadian people. It is the Liberal ethic, and your practice, to promise the earth and to deliver nothing. And when ordinary Canadians realize they have been conned and short-changed, they go after their Provincial officials, if only for the reasons that they are the closest people to get back at, and they don't know how to reach the federal wrong–doers who are the authors of their misfortune and disillusionment.

Trickery? Scam? I'll say. Well over one hundred BILLION dollars in public taxation funds is spent every year on health throughout Canada. And what do we get for it? It is a system in disarray. Ordinary Canadians have to wait a good two years in most parts of Canada for a hip replacement, for example. What if you, Jean–Joseph, needed a hip replacement? How long would you have to wait? Probably two days. You remind me of Stalin's Communist society, where all are equal. Except that some are more equal than others. You are like the rulers of the Taliban of Afghanistan, who outlawed television and good foods and sex, and who in their protected strongholds enjoyed all of those things in secrecy. It was ever thus. You are no different from other autocrats: you preach one thing, to the populace and live the high life with your buddies of the Shawinigan Golf Club and Bombardier and Groupaction advertising agency.

You and your fellow-socialists of the New Democratic Party have carried out a campaign to convince Canadians that health is the most important thing they can have and the most important thing that government can do for them. These claims are demonstrable untruths. But Canadians have bought into it, and you knew they would. For the clear truth is that the single most important thing in any society – on a par with national security and a sound currency – is EDUCATION. I do not need to challenge you to ask Canadians which is the more important. It is easy to demonstrate. If all hospitals, for example, were to close overnight, what would the social damage be? If all schools and universities were to close overnight, what would the damage be? There is no comparison.

But you know, we all know, and above all everyone knows how you think and act: namely, there are votes in health, there are no votes in education. That is the sum and substance of your political life. You want another instance of the political mind at work? Look at our modern hospitals: they are palatial edifices. And our modern schools? Like rabbit hutches. Yet hospital patients are transient visitors. Even doctors and nurses and laboratory technicians come and go with some frequency. But schools are permanent: the pupils spend up to twelve years in one school; and teachers might spend thirty years at one place of work. Look at the schools built in the 1930s, 1940s and even 1950s: they are monuments to good architecture and to what is permanent in our lives.

Even the title, Department of Health, is misleading, if you examine it.. You and your political colleagues are not concerned with health. The departments should be named in accordance with their true function, namely, with sickness, disease, illness, and death. All the talk we, the deceived public, ever hear from you and your political ilk has to do with waiting lists, the shortage of hospital beds, the reluctance of doctors to live and practice in rural towns, the lack of money for this and that. It will be a frosty Friday, the day when we hear a politician come clean and show their real concern with health, and show us the efforts they are making to combat obesity, to reduce the carnage on our roads, to combat alcoholism and drug addiction, to encourage a healthy life style. What, for example, is being done in our schools? Of course you don't know! Education is nothing to do with the federal government. What is clear is that you pick and choose among the public concerns, according as to whether there is any political gain in it for you.

If there is one health issue that hits the headlines in our newspapers nearly every day, both here at home and in other countries, it is the scourge of AIDS. What have you ever done about that pandemic, other than preach to others, and to offer a few million dollars, and urge others to take action? You remember the sudden scare caused by SARS, don't you? What did you do about it? Your department, waiting as they were for a word of leadership from you, bungled the thing, because you were on holiday and couldn't be bothered with it. Eventually, some medical authorities in Ontario began to take action. Among the measures taken was the extreme precaution of quarantining people who had symptoms of the disease, or who been in contact with people who had the symptoms. Of course, SARS was, from the very beginning, an infectious disease that afflicted very few people; and among those infected, only a tiny number died.

But what of AIDS? If ever there was a ghastly and deadly disease, one that was easily transmissible, it is AIDS. If ever there was a pandemic that demanded that the infected be quarantined, this was it. What did you do? Absolutely nothing! And why? Because it was clear from the beginning that AIDS was being transmitted, in its early manifestation, largely by male homosexuals; and, also that it was of African origin. So, from this twofold motive, you went out of your way to avoid offending male homosexuals in our society and third world countries while putting all Canadians at enormous risk to their health and lives. I challenge you to explain this dereliction of duty, this crime against humanity.

Whatever the answer, what is clear is that by taking the measures that the situation called for, both in Canada and in other countries, you could have saved millions of lives and spared thousands of Canadian families untold misery and anguish. But, as I have accused you before, so I accuse you now, once again, Jean–Joseph, of appearing not to have an iota of humanity in your make–up.

Not the least of your offences against the people of Canada is your boneheaded ideological hostility to any form of private medicine. You parrot the socialist mantra that private medicine is medicine "for profit" – implying, and at times shouting, that the medical profession is out to make unwarranted financial gain *at the expense of the public*. And yet you and your socialist supporters are only too keen to rush to a doctor at the onset of the merest twinge. Twinge of the body, yes, but not twinge of the conscience, for the reason that you are devoid of conscience, as you are deficient in morality and decency.

The Canada Health Act has been the greatest vote-getter of all time for the federal Liberal Party. They know it and they have milked it for all it's worth. It has finally become blindingly clear to all reasonable people that the health care system with its five 'principles' is not sustainable. Over one hundred BILLION dollars a year is being sucked up by the system, and the system is getting worse by the month. (In some provinces, up to 40% of its annual wealth is being squandered on health. This figure represents a monstrous dereliction of their duty by the provincial and federal politicians.)

It is possible that the architects and administrators of the Act knew or suspected at the time that it would prove to be unworkable. Whether they knew and said nothing, or whether they did not know and did not care to find out at the time, its authors are equally guilty of a massive fraud against the Canadian people. Something has to go. The Romanow Commission was a wasteful exercise in ideological flim-flam, its conclusions set down before any evidence was heard. Some influential people have to take the lead in deciding which of the principles entrenched in the Canada Health Act have to be jettisoned or severely curtailed. In a word, which services will continue to be provided, and which abandoned.

The prohibition against citizens wishing to spend their own money on obtaining health services from private sources is preposterous. (Oh, I was forgetting: private, for-profit abortion clinics are ok.) Talk about morality! Yes, talking about morality. We read in John Ivison's report (*National Post,* Jan. 31) on the Premiers' conference on health this ringing declaration: "[Prime Minister Paul] Martin said yesterday he accepted the principle of the Romanow commission, which argued medicare is a moral enterprise, not a business one..." This distinction implies a divorce between ethics and business. As the owner of a vast shipping company, Mr. Martin presumably knows what he is talking about.

On the other hand, if ethics, or simple principles of accounting and accountability, are left out of the equation of the finances underpinning the health system, is it any wonder that a) the health care system has become unsustainable, and b) no politician or bureaucrat is prepared to bite the bullet and say so? P.S. This last statement reminds us of Paul Martin's campaign against Jean Chrétien. He carried it out by using Chrétien's own choice methods of subterfuge, trickery and deceit. He shied away, like a coward, from confronting him. We are also reminded that while Martin was the Finance Minister, during the years 1993 to 2001, his wealthy company applied for and received at least $10.3 million in grants from his own government. It also appears that his company received hundreds of millions of dollars' worth of contracts during the same period. That's not bad going for a company registered outside Canada, so as to avoid taxes, safety regulations, and union dues, and for a company president who electioneers on a platform of social welfare. (Pssst! Are Canadian voters listening, or are they mostly still asleep, or just calmly figuring which Party is promising them most?)

CHILDREN AND YOUTH

This is as good a place as any to introduce a word about children. The fact that there is a federal ministry of Children and Youth at all demonstrates as clearly as can be the persistent ethos of interference into provincial and municipal affairs that prevails in the Byzantine alleyways of Liberal Ottawa. And even worse, the intrusion into the lives of individual Canadians and Canadian families by the Chrétien ghouls who inhabit them.

A case in point is the charge before an Ontario court against a parent who spanked his child. I concede there are no problem children, only problem parents and problem teachers. And problem social workers, politicians and judges in the hundreds.

I have challenged before and I will challenge again: I'll wager that not one Liberal MP in a hundred can name the present minister for Children and Youth. And I'll wager that you, Jean-Joseph, have not spoken to the minister about his or her portfolio in the past six months, if that.

Talking about wagers: I'll bet you remember the occasion, a few years ago, in South-East Asia, on one of your expensive and futile trade mission boondoggles, when you were suddenly confronted by a Canadian boy who challenged you to do something about child labour in Asia. You, and indeed the whole Canadian delegation, were rocked back on your collective heels. Why? Because you had never thought about it and had no principles. You uttered some pious platitudes, thanked the young man for his social concern, and promised to look into it. Of course, night turned into day, and you not only forgot about him, but deliberately forgot what you had said to him.

No one can fail to salute anyone moved to relieve suffering and to better people's lives, especially the young and defenseless. Craig Keilberger is a nice young man, and sincere, but it seems to me that he was mistaken in an important way. He was, it seems, primordially concerned with child slavery. It is of the greatest importance to distinguish between necessary child labour and child slave-labour. Many thousands of children in India, Pakistan, Bangladesh, and elsewhere have to work, in order to scrape together a subsistence living. But -- and this is equally important -- they are learning a trade which will enable them to support themselves and their families well into the future, and perhaps lay the foundations, built upon progressively, which will last a lifetime. And a trade useful to society, because necessary. Craig reminds me a little -- and I don't want to be unkind -- of that wonderful scene in *Bleak House*. Mrs. Jellaby's upstairs flat is a chaos of screaming, hungry and fighting children, while she sits serenely undisturbed at the kitchen table writing letters to important people begging for funds to alleviate hunger and social disorder in Africa. Yet I take my hat off to

Craig. He wants to do something for others. And there are too many hundreds of thousands of people who opt out of their social obligations, preferring to let others do it. They figure that if they donate a few dollars a year to some 'good cause' -- like a hospital -- they have done their civic duty. Especially if they get a tax deductible receipt for their money.

I ask our young friend to look around him, here in Canada. He will see many thousands of young people, even children, who are working in all kinds of jobs. They deliver papers and pizzas. They wash cars. They work in clothing stores, in fast-food outlets, in eateries, in video stores, in cinemas, in music stores, in snack-bars, at street food wagons...you name it. I once came across a young boy who was working as a bus-boy in a restaurant, clearing dirty dishes. I asked him why he was working, and not studying or playing with friends? His reply was that he had to buy a pair of goalie's pads if he wanted to be selected for his school team. "How much do the pads cost?" -- "Eight hundred dollars." The question arises: Do they have to work? I mean, in the sense that those poor Indian children have to work? The answer is a shattering NO!. They work for the sole reason that they want to have money to spend. Spend on what? Spend

on CDs and rock concerts, clothes, and booze --
and perhaps drugs. That reason is not a reason.
And hockey pads is not a sufficient reason
either. If abuse of children means anything, it is
the employment of children for reasons other
than necessity. Our children should not, ever,
be employed for gain, for the mere reason that
they want money to spend on frivolous things,
on trivialities, on services and products that
they have no business hankering after at their
age. The most despicable sight of all, in the
sphere of child labour, is their exploitation in
advertising, on television and radio and in the
press. Advertising as practised today is a
powerful engine of consumerism, and one of our
pervasive modern social evils. If children are to
be employed at all, it should be solely in the
arts, the creative and the interpretative arts.
And the moneys they earn should be held in a
trust until they are 21, and only those sums
used before then that are necessary for their
art. Craig, where are you? You, Jean-Joseph,
we know where you are.

FINANCES
        There is no area of responsible
government that should take precedence over
defence and security, but it is evident that
finance is an equally vital partner in the totality

of public policy. Without finance, that is, without the necessary revenues from all sources, no provision can be made for the vital services that all governments must provide to the citizens of their country.

What do I mean by Finance? I mean, the very complicated matters of revenue and expenditures. In this discussion I will not touch on taxation. Here I am concerned solely with expenditures. Expenditure implies priorities. Priorities must be established by Cabinet–not by the whim of an autocratic prime minister. It is abundantly clear that some ministries require more funds than others. That is the task of Cabinet to decide. To decide according to a national system of priorities.

Often we hear these 'soulful' plaints from government spokesmen – of all governments, in every part of the country: "We do not have the money." Or: "The money is not there." Or: "We didn't budget for that item." Confront them, I say! They are not telling the truth. Of course the money is there. Look at the annual budget. In the case of the federal government, the annual budget amounts to about one hundred and eighty BILLION dollars. Where does the money go? What is it spent on? Who gets it?

The excuse that you don't have the money for this or that urgent or vital need is a shameful deceit perpetrated upon the Canadian taxpaying public. If you were to tell the truth for once you would say this: "It is true that we have the money. After all, look at our annual budget – it is something like one hundred and eighty billion dollars a year But we, I mean I, choose not to put any money into that project or programme for the simple reason – and I have done a lot of calculating – either that there are no votes in it for us, or I am determined to ruin the efficiency of – just to take an example out of thin air – our Armed Forces."

According to both custom and tradition – and even more importantly, for reasons of ethical and responsible and accountable government – the Government of the day is duty bound to bring down a Budget every year. That Budget will report on the revenues that the Government expects to receive, and the expenditures they may legitimately expect to have to meet in the course of their commitments.

You, Jean–Joseph Chrétien, have been at pains to avoid bringing down budgets, in defiance of necessity. You have constantly avoided answering specific questions in the

House. Every year, for the ten years of your prime ministership, the Auditor General has presented a report to Parliament, which has been highly critical of your Government and of both its spending and accounting practices. The Auditor General has made specific allegations of malpractice in various departments. In more than one instance, he or she has stated that a certain Department's accounting practices have deviated so radically from normal responsible accounting procedures, that it has been impossible to present a reliable and final account.

I could itemize the monstrous irregularities perpetrated within the various departments of your Government. Let anyone read the Auditor General's annual reports. The clear fact is established beyond doubt that you and your colleagues, with your consent and following your example, have spent billions of dollars which are unaccounted for – and which are unaccounted for precisely because you and your associates have made sure that they will never be found. I can cite one instance – and it must be one instance among many: You established a secret trust fund in Quebec, out of public funds, a fund worth seven billion dollars, perhaps with Cabinet approval but certainly without Parliament's knowledge, for purposes that are known but that will never be publicly declared.

For the past several years the Opposition parties and the Press have exposed monstrous scandals and excesses in departments of your government. Your response? You have invariably cried, either, 'We are not perfect, we will try to do better', or, 'That is not within my area of responsibility. That is a matter for...' – and you either point the finger at a Cabinet colleague – i.e. an appointed bootlicker – or a senior civil servant. Or, a big corporation that receives millions of dollars' worth of contracts from you, and which, in return, donates millions of dollars to the Liberal party of Canada.

There have been monstrous scams within the numerous branches of your government in the past ten years. The greatest scam of all is the gun registration scandal. Originally it was announced as being self-financing, i.e. the registration fees would cover the administrative costs of running the programme. You – yes, you, Jean–Joseph Chrétien – were personally informed that this announcement was not honest. Yet you persisted in it. Why? Because you saw in it the very real likelihood of tapping into a source of public support. In a word, you saw in it a source of votes. And what has happened? What has happened is what your critics suspected would happen – in other words, the gun registration bureaucratic jungle has run into a cost over-run that even you did not envisage. So far, this monstrous waste of public funds has run into the staggering figure of over ONE BILLION DOLLARS. And it has not contributed one single solitary iota to the realization of its stated purpose. And what is the whole purpose of your gun registration programme? Why, it is to make Canadians safer. What a farce! Are you stupid or something? Since when did criminals register their weapons? Since when did law-abiding citizens who owned rifles use them to commit crimes? Their rifles were registered anyway. Now that you have seen for yourself that this programme has turned out to be a vast waste of tax moneys and human resources, what is your response? Why, you claim that you had no idea that it would cost so much; that it is not your business, but the responsibility of the Attorney-General; and that it is doing what it was set up to do anyway.

You could also have said, 'Well, we are not perfect, we will try to do better.' And what was your actual reaction? Why, you laid it on the Attorney General to demand more funds from Parliament, on the ground that the programme was working so well that it needed only a few more hundreds of millions of dollars to be perfect, and to do away with all gun–related crimes in Canada. And what did the Attorney General do? And what did the Cabinet do? Why, they tugged their individual and collective forelocks enough, and they acquiesced in every ukase issuing from on high, from the PMO or even higher. I can readily imagine you, Jean–Joseph, mounted on your elevated seat in the Berchtesgarten, and sending forth decrees hither and yon, with a wilful and dangerous disregard of truth, decency and national security.

It is notorious, nay, it is infamous in any country outside of Zimbabwe, that you should shovel out funds in the billions according to one over–riding principle. (I realize that the very idea of your name and administration being linked with anything resembling principles is hilarious, but there you are.) The principle is this: you disburse public moneys to those who can do the most for you politically in return. One example: a leading Canadian magazine was approached with an offer to carry out an investigation into your government's $3 billion infrastructure programme to determine how much was spent on legitimate public projects, and how much of it was surreptitiously siphoned off into Liberal ridings. The offer was spurned with indifference. Was that magazine receiving subsidies from 'Culture' Copps, with your blessing?

One of the most generously subsidized corporations in Canada is, not surprisingly, located in Quebec. It is Bombardier, which makes aircraft and trains. (Is there a family connection between you and their president?) Despite the billions of public funds poured into that company, it is still only barely solvent. Among the subsidies, and unreturnable 'loans', you have lavished on Bombardier, there is a small item of $87 million from the Technology Partnership Loans between 1996 and 2000. Of that, $411,000 has been contributed to the Liberal Party of Canada in the form of a political donation. That is to say, that moneys have been diverted, with only one small intermediate step, from public funds into a private organization. Where the money goes to from that political party is anyone's guess. But we all have our well founded ideas, don't we, Jean–Joseph?

Other vast sums of public moneys have gone to such impoverished corporations as IBM,

Pratt and Whitney, and SNC Lavelin. Are they all in Quebec, or in Liberal ridings, or generous donors to the Liberal Party? That is not the end of it, is it, Jean-Joseph? For several years snippets of information have leaked out to the press that numerous high ranking civil servants have been travelling on long overseas trips for various purposes, such as purchasing commissions and international conferences, and charging to the public purse vast sums in expenses. Even worse, it is rumoured that senior civil servants have been entertaining people at the swankiest restaurants in Ottawa and Montreal, and even including expensive wines at public expense.

At the moment of writing – and we are now in October 2003 – the scandal of George Radwanski, the Privacy Commissioner, has hit the headlines. He and his top associate have charged to the public accounts huge bills for lavish living for themselves and guests in Ottawa, and the Auditor-General – who seems to be one of the few honest and ethical people in Ottawa, and indeed in the whole galimaufry of senior *apparatchik* – has castigated him for offences that have resulted in the calling in of the RCMP to investigate. But, hey, what the heck – he's a Liberal isn't he? A pal of yours, isn't he? Or at least he's your nominee for past services. But that's what happens to your people who get caught, right? You throw them to the wolves. Who's next?

Now again, the hard news has been confirmed that a large number of the top bureaucrats in National Defence have been living high off the hog all over the world on dubious junkets. In National Defence, of all departments of government. The Army, the Air Force and the Navy have been screaming for funds for the whole period of your premiership. And for that entire period of ten years you – yes, you, Jean–Joseph – have been cutting back and cutting back. It has been a constant policy of cut, slash and burn. And here we have your top civil servants in National Defence going off on lavish, expense-paid international travels. And for what purpose? Just listen to this. "Military officials – read: civilian officials working for the military – say (their) expenses are necessary for the high–level bureaucrats to carry out such tasks as attending international conferences and visiting suppliers of equipment." Read it carefully: they use the same self-serving, hifalutin language as you do when you are evasive. "Tasks", for one. That suggests hard work. What, at conferences? Conferences, especially international conferences, are nothing but an excuse for having a good time at public expense with a minimum of work. And, assuredly, with nothing accomplished that could not have been done by mail or telephone. And what about this: "visiting suppliers of equipment"? I ask you, what equipment? Outworn submarines? Rusty Volkswagen jeeps? Spare parts for 35 year old helicopters? And when a decision is finally made for this or that purchase, it is calculated that the process has cost far more than the equipment.

But we're forgetting something in this tally – we're forgetting the travel expenses. High–flying bureaucrats – some of the names (and we're talking only of the Department of National Defence) are Evelyne Levine, Alan Williams, Margaret Bloodworth and Doug Drever–racked up vast expenses for first class travel, posh hotels, and the best restaurants and wines, while the Armed Forces were deprived of a decent wage or being killed in foreign lands for want of proper equipment; and while those at home living in DND houses have their rents jacked up far beyond their increases in pay.

And what about staff? You have padded the pay-rolls with employees, mostly from Quebec, so that a bureacracy numbering thirteen thousand pen-pushers and committee-men are needed to administer

Armed Forces numbering only sixty-five thousand.

Back to Bombardier. You bought two luxury aircraft from them at a cost of one hundred million dollars, for the sole purpose of shoring up their finances and giving you or allowing you to fly on foreign junkets in great luxury. The aircraft were not needed, according to your own experts; they were not tendered for, as the law requires; and you spend, on a personal whim, one hundred million dollars, while men and women of our Armed Forces are being killed for want of decent equipment, and while Canadian citizens are dying prematurely for want of medical attention. Your villainy knows no bounds.

QUÉBEC

Any such survey as this of your years as Prime Minister would be incomplete without an examination, however brief, of Quebec's place in Canada, and of your Government's policy towards Quebec and its relations with Canada.

Ever since the Trudeau years there has been a lamentable, and damaging, split between Quebec (plus Ontario) and all of Western Canada. Trudeau was the author of this terrible development in Canadian affairs, and you,

Jean–Joseph, not only did nothing to repair the damage, you went out of your way to exacerbate it. Your entire political life has been centred on votes in Quebec and Ontario, and among the ethnic minorities whom you have encouraged to enter Canada.

You have known all along that for a very large number of Canadians of Western Canada – and I am talking about all of Canada from Manitoba to the Pacific Coast – Canada would be well rid of Quebec. Canada would prosper and be truly united without the burden of Quebec.

You know this. You have been aware all your political life that your province of Québec has been like a burr under the saddle of our Canadian Confederation. For more years than most Canadians can recall, there has been an underlying spirit of nationalistic secession among a sizeable proportion of the people of Québec. I have personally met such individuals: one, a sergeant then in the former Royal Canadian Air Force back in 1958 – though what on earth a separatist was doing in the RCAF I can't imagine; and, in 1978, a student in France.

The sole bouquet I will hand to you, Jean–Joseph, is for your work to prevent the secession of Québec. I pointedly avoided saying, "to keep Canada whole and united", for this was not your aim or purpose. Your interest in Canada was as a platform for your political ambitions. I have no doubt that if your political ambitions could have been realized by promoting Québec's national and sovereigntist agenda, you would have been in provincial politics and not federal. But there was much more to be gained in federal politics.

Your overt policies to keep Québec within the Canadian Confederation have centred largely on uncontrolled and vast handouts in the billions of dollars to Québec industries and other interests; and on restricting trade within Canada to the advantage of Québec.

It is, for example, an utter disgrace that free trade does not exist between the Provinces within Canada. Quebec interests – among which we note especially the dairy industry – call the shots. And yet you have taken measures to further the interests of Québec nationalism. Your Liberal Party of Canada disgraced itself a few years ago by according the right – note: the right – of Québec to secede from Canada. (The fact that the then Progressive Conservative Party of Canada and the NDP did the same thing does not justify or confirm the rightness of your act: it merely served to intensify the crime.) One cannot conceive the same thing happening in the United States. There, there would be war before any state could secede. In Canada, apparently, Canada is of such little importance that a political leader can connive in its fragmentation.

The act of the Liberal Party is one thing. But you went further. You, Jean–Joseph, went so far as to enact a Bill, which clarified the terms according to which the secession of Québec was made possible. In ancient law there are pretty strong terms for abetting the dissolution of a country. (Note that, for some people, the secession of Québec would be a sort of liberation for Canada as a whole; whereas the same act would be rather the ruination of Canada.)

The fundamental error and aotucratic high-handedness of which I accuse you, Jean–Joseph, is that you have always regarded Québec and its relations with Canada as a matter solely for the federal government to decide. Québec is but one of a number of Provinces. Each Province is a part of the whole, which is the Confederation. It is not possible for Québec alone, or the Government of Canada alone, or of the two governments, to decide the

fate of Canada and Québec. The whole of
Canada is involved. The only way in which the
fate and future of Québec, as of Canada, can be
decided, is by recourse to the judgement of all
Canadians. And there exist only two methods of
determining that judgement: by a general
election, or by a binding referendum. It was
absolutely essential that, before Québec held
a referendum, the federal Government hold a
national referendum on that one issue. If the
result was Yes, then Québec would be expelled
from Confederation. If the result was No, then
the question of Québec secession would never
again be raised. And for evermore Québec,
subject only to the preservation of her language
and laws, would be treated by Ottawa and the
other Provinces as one of them, and without any
other special privileges.

NATIONAL DEFENCE

In May 1995 I was at Groesbeek, in
Holland, to participate in the ceremonies
organized by the Dutch Government and people
to celebrate the 50th anniversary of the
liberation of the Dutch people from the German
conquest and occupation in the Second World
War. Groesbeek is the site of the largest
Canadian Military Cemetery in Europe. That is
where the major ceremony took place. You were
there too. I saw you, and I heard you. It was the

Dutch Prime Minister who gave the first eulogy. His speech was a moving, and eloquent, reminder of the horrors of war, of the suffering of the Dutch people, and above all, of the eternal debt they owed to Canada and the Canadian Armed Forces for their liberation. And following their liberation, for the example of decency and humanity the soldiers and airmen showed to the people of Holland. Never have I heard such an outpouring of gratitude expressed formally and officially by a government head to a foreign people, in the presence of the head of government of that other people. I do not believe than many such utterances exist in the world's annals.

You spoke next. Do you remember what you said? I don't expect you do. But I do. What you said was unforgettable. You uttered a string of platitudes about the valour of the Canadian Forces, with your voice an expressionless drone of insincerity. You even managed to insert a partisan political note about the government of the day. In closing, you did at least put a bit of life into your words when you proclaimed: "We were proud of you. We will never forget you!"

The point is of course that everything you said was calculated, and not believed by you for an instant. The fact is that you were addressing a large gathering of veterans. And what would a statement reeking of insincerity cost you? No one would remember it. But I remember it. And I accuse you, Jean–Joseph, of the cruellest and most cynical utterance in a long career of cynical deceit. You have made similar remarks at some of Canada's most solemn occasions, such as the Remembrance Day services at the Cenotaph in Ottawa. And your hypocrisy and insincerity have been equally evident.

Now, today, in October 2003, the pigeons are coming home to roost. Your servile Veterans' Affairs minister has announced that the pensions of some twenty–three thousand veterans' widows will be cut off. The widows of veterans. The very men to whom you have given solemn pledges over the years. "We will never forget you!" What a diabolical piece of duplicity and mendacity.

This heartless decision caused a storm of protest throughout the country. The Opposition Party challenged the Veterans' Affairs minister. Who is he? Does anyone know? Can anyone name him? Or find him? Well, the Loyal Opposition found him, when the Disloyal Government couldn't. His name is Rey Pagtakhan. He was forced to defend 'his' decision, and explain 'his' policy. This is one of his most comprehensive statements:

> "It was not for lack of heart. It was for the reality of limited resources at the time. The dilemma we have is that we have limited resources."

I accuse you, Rey Pagtakhan, of a gross lie. Of course the money is there. Your department and other departments spend vast sums every month on trivialities, on junkets, and on vote-buying schemes. And you have the gall to lie in the face of 23,000 widows whom you are depriving of a bare subsistence pension? What you avoided saying, in your devious political way, as nearly all politicians say, is this: 'Sure, the money is there, but we have more important things to spend it on.' You also said: "This issue of extending the benefits to all the widows certainly will continue to be an issue and will be in the heart of this Minister." How brazen can one get?

The storm finally broke over your head, reaching even into the deep recesses of the riding of Shawinigan. You, Jean-Joseph, poked your head out of your bolt-hole and pledged that you would review the situation. But we know your pledges. They are like your election promises, like your vows and oaths of office. A month later you have still refused to set a date for when you will act. And the widows are waiting. You had better not hold your breath, Widows. Just remember the words of the most honest, caring Prime Minister you have ever had: "I will never forget you!"

The scenario is easy to re-create. The question of the widows' pensions comes up. Pagtakhan has to make a decision. No, that's wrong. Pagtakhan has to have a decision made for him. So he dutifully – love that word: 'dutifully'! – that is, servilely slinks round to your Office of a hundred–plus carefully selected acolytes, and begs for a word. One of the Top Honchos either comes to a decision on his own, or telephones *le gros Fromage* for the word. Pagtakhan slinks back to his office, and is ready for his sob story when the Opposition or the press questions him again. When the heat gets hotter, the faithful and 'dutiful' minister gets on his knees to you. You, out of extraordinary, even supererogatory, clemency and mansuetude, step into the breech to rescue your faithful servant. With a hollow promise.

The other scenario – the behind-the-scenes scenario – is equally easy to re-create. Your faithful Veterans' Affairs minister seeks your decision, as you knew he would, about pensions for the twenty-three thousand widows. You tell him your decision, arrived at long ago: "No way! No money!" Pagtakhan takes the heat, as you knew he would. Pagtakhan is besieged, and looks up at you for rescue, as you knew he would. You step into the breach, and announce loudly and publicly that you will personally look into the situation and see if it can't be revised, hoping that the furor will die down and eventually be forgotten, by both a tired Opposition and a cynical press. Which you know it will. And you will have saved the government a few measly millions of dollars so that you and all the other Members of Parliament can enjoy your doubled salaries and tripled pensions.

Let us turn to today's Armed Forces, and the men and women who "stand on guard" for their country so nobly. (But they had better be warned what to expect when they become veterans, if the Liberal Party still calls the shots in Ottawa.) You have corrupted the Armed Forces of Canada by a process of politicization just as you have debased other formerly great Canadian institutions. I refer to the Royal Canadian Mounted Police, the Canadian Broadcasting Corporation, the Canadian Film Board, the Canada Council, the Canadian Council on Broadcasting Services, to name a few – and not forgetting the very judiciary system and its principles that you are sworn to uphold.

How have you corrupted them? By a number of ways. I shall limit myself to the Armed Forces; but what I shall say of them will apply to the others, some if not all.

You have integrated the civilian and military upper echelons of the Ministry of National Defence in Ottawa so that the civilian bureaucrats outnumber the Service members by four or five to one in all the important committees, thus ensuring political control, since the minister and 90% of civil servants in Ottawa vote for the Liberal Party. There have been no fewer than five ministers of National Defence during your prime ministership. The changeovers are part and parcel of your secret agenda of never letting any minister remain long enough in any department lest he learn to understand its real needs and, perhaps, come under the influence of its senior army, navy and air force officers. That would be intolerable. So you appoint wimps. And the moment they begin to show a few signs of independence, you get rid of them.

Look at the present incumbent. And weep! What's his name? Ah, yes, the eminently forgettable, and spineless, John McCallum. He makes a statement, when cornered by the press, and the next day you issue a statement contradicting him. And does this McCallum resign? Of course not! Why? Because he is too keen on his perks and privileges. And do you replace him for uttering false or misleading statements? Of course not! Why, the next time, you might really get an unsuspected free thinker. McCallum you can control. That's all you want.

For the past several years, our Armed Forces have been enveloped in scandal over the lack of equipment and over faulty equipment. The scandal has been one of your making. Not only that, but of your deliberate and wilful making. Yet you hesitate not a second to take decisions out of the hands of the Minister of National Defence and commit men and women of the defence forces to dangerous parts of the world on so-called peace-keeping assignments, with a total and callous disregard for their safety. With the inevitable consequence that many of our brave and dedicated men and women have been killed for lack of equipment or for having defective equipment. What is important to you is to strut the world stage and to appear to be doing something 'important' in the eyes of the world.

The latest outrage is the death of two of our soldiers in Afghanistan. You, Jean-Joseph, ordered two thousand Canadian Army men and women to Afghanistan on a dangerous, and essentially fruitless mission, for one reason and one reason only: to satisfy your vanity and lust for control. For the fact is that Afghanistan means nothing to us, and we have no business there. Our Armed Forces exist either for war or for peace keeping. This operation is neither: it is a policing action. There is a big difference; and you neither know nor care.

Those two soldiers, Sergeant Robert Short and Corporal Robbie Beerenfenger, were buried on October 7th in a military ceremony at their home base of Canadian Forces Base Petawawa, Pembroke, Ontario. Their families issued a statement saying that they did not want you, or the minister for defence, or even the Chief of the General Staff, to attend. If ever there was a slap in the face for you, Jean-Joseph, coming from a patriotic Canadian family, that was it.

The Commander of the Army, Lieutenant-General Rick Hillier, delivered the address. His address was eloquent, as befits a high-ranking officer. It was courageous, as befits a soldier with a courage that has been entirely lacking in the politically correct upper echelons of the military brass for many years. I am obliged to reprint here a long excerpt from it.

COMMANDER'S SPEECH

<u>The very best citizens our country has to offer</u>

It is the soldier, not the journalist, who guarantees freedom of speech; it is the soldier, not the politician, who guarantees our democracy; it is the soldier, not the diplomat, that becomes the tangible expression of our nation's beliefs and extends its values and its ideals worldwide; and it is the soldier, whose flag-draped coffin vividly demonstrates the ultimate cost of representing our beliefs in difficult and dangerous places.

The honourable profession of a soldier in Canada's army is exciting, challenging and rewarding, but extremely demanding. The great men and women who wear our nation's uniform so proudly have become our very best credentials around the world, representing all 31 million Canadians outside their own country, but sometimes under appreciated here in Canada, they are held to exacting standards... and as we sadly remember today, a level of risk that can mean their very lives. Those soldiers miss births and birthdays; first words and first steps. They miss a spouse's excitement, weddings, anniversaries and

sometimes even the opportunity to say goodbye to
loved ones because of the work they do. The ultimate
compliment we can offer each, would be to call them
quite simply, Canadian soldiers. The kind of people
who volunteer to become soldiers, and take up those
daunting challenges, represent–as did Sergeant Short
and Corporal Beerenfenger–the very best citizens our
country has to offer. Hard as nails on the outside, a
soft touch for all on the inside... men who did not see
things in the terrible way that they are and ask: 'why?'
but men who could see things as they should be and
simply ask 'why not?'...These were practical people,
who acted when others talked about acting. But it
would he wrong to describe them as supermen,
because they were not. They simply were ordinary
Canadians,   who   used   their   devotion   and
determination to accomplish extraordinary things on a
daily basis. They have continued the valorous tradition
of Canadian soldiers. The soldiers volunteer for this
tough profession, they know the risks but they also
know that even with the sacrifices, their commitment
means something. They know and believe that their
presence and work represents the difference between
life and death, hope and despair to countless
thousands around the world ... in places where our
privileged life in Canada is but a dream. They loved
what they were doing and they were brave in the
execution of their duties, and for that we are so proud
of them, Canadian heroes in a world desperately in
need of them...For (their wives and families and their
children) words cannot convey adequately the
gratitude of a nation and offer appreciation for being
the strength to help us get through this week.

How were these two men killed? They
were killed when the vehicle in which they were
patrolling in Afghanistan ran over a landmine.
The vehicle is called the "Iltis". It is built by

Volkswagen. And that tells us much of what we need to know. The story of the decision to purchase this vehicle rather than any other, among a number of superior, vehicles, is just one of the countless black marks against your name and which will be counted in the tally of your legacy.

The simple fact is that there existed already three combat vehicles, proven in the field by several armies, and which were in production. At the time of the decision, the then minister, one Eggleton – whom you subsequently dismissed for giving an untendered contract to a friend, as he thought it ok to do since he was only following your example – decided that there had to be a Canadian firm that produced a vehicle that would pass muster, even if it wasn't up to the requirements of our military. The firm was found. You instructed the weapons procurement branch to change the specifications of the vehicle so that the Canadian company could enter a bid. When the other three firms found out what they were up against they withdrew. Eventually the Canadian company withdrew its bid as well. And our Armed Forces were saddled with a totally inferior and inadequate vehicle for carrying out dangerous patrols and reconnaissance.

Your role in this murderous business is plain for all to see. For the established fact is that, from the moment you became Prime Minister in 1993, you placed an embargo on military acquisitions and modernization. You ordered unilaterally a reduction of the budget of the Armed Forces by 25%, and the supine Cabinet went along with it.

"The tale of the Iltis is hardly unique," reports the *National Post* of October 15. "Nearly every weapons system, vehicle, aircraft and ship still in use by the Canadian military tells the same woeful tale. Two-thirds of our fighter jets are grounded for lack of spare parts and mechanics, and those still in the air have on-board computers that go back to the age of Pong. Our main battle tank is of the same era as those formerly possessed by Iraq's Republican Guard. Our troops in Afghanistan went nearly two years without desert uniforms. So many of our aging maritime patrol craft are in hangars for repair at any one time that large swaths of our coastline are unguarded despite increasing terror threats and rampant people-smuggling. Our air force has so few troop carriers that when Governor-General Adrienne Clarkson recently tied up one of its planes to go jet-setting around northern Europe at taxpayer expense with a five-dozen strong retinue in tow, while troops due for rotation out after a six-month peacekeeping mission to Bosnia had to wait days for a flight back to Canada.

And then, of course, there are Canada's "'60s-era Sea King helicopters. By all known engineering standards, these obsolete rust-buckets should have been sold for scrap years ago. But you personally, dictatorially, cancelled a contract for a new maritime helicopter in 1993. (The move was designed to save cash. But ironically, the resultant cancellation penalties and maintenance contracts cost as much as Ottawa would have paid for new helicopters.) The vehicles are so old that each requires an average of 30 man-hours of repairs for every hour of flight time. In February, a Sea King fell 10 metres on to the deck of a destroyer–the latest in a long line of mishaps. One can only hope none of our troops die in Sea Kings between now and the time they are eventually replaced. But if tragedy does strike in coming years, critics may be able to point to the same politicking that has marred the search for an Iltis replacement. Earlier this year, accusations surfaced that process for a new helicopter had been dumbed down to favour a French company after Raymond Chrétien, your nephew and then our ambassador to France, held a private meeting with company officials. The two-engined French product is less safe than the three-engined models offered by competitors. But no matter. To the Liberals, French demands apparently take precedence over our troops' safety.

In December 2001, Canada's Auditor-General estimated that $5-billion was needed just to keep the Armed Forces mission-ready. The Liberals instead promised $1.6 billion over five years. That quickly fell to $1.2 billion. And even that amount has since disappeared. Since the end of 2001, Ottawa has found only $300million ~ $500million for new military equipment, no more than 10% of the minimum specified by the senior officers' latest expert requirements .

I recall the moment, about two years ago, when you uttered the solemn pronouncement: "If you want peace, prepare for war!" You spouted this ancient maxim because it sounded good - a bit like Trudeau's notorious and phoney aphorism: "The universe is unfolding as it should." And of course the press, and perhaps even their fellow-Liberals, were suitably bemused! Of course Trudeau uttered his mantra without believing it for a moment. But you spouted your proverb as if you believed it and had no intention of doing anything about it, even though it cost the lives of many of our soldiers and airmen.

Following in the footsteps of the dilettante, pseudo–philosopher, spend–happy, Castro-admirer Trudeau, you have demonstrated a hatred of the Canadian Armed Forces, and have taken every measure possible to reduce them to impotence. But one thing you have not been able to touch is their methods of training.

The happy fact is that our Armed Forces, Navy, Army and Air Force, have maintained their British traditions of discipline, customs and integrity. Even the politicization of the top echelons has not been able to prevent the continued liaison of our Forces with the British. We cooperate naturally with the British Armed Forces, rather than with the American, outside the defensive theatre of North America. Read again the address of Lt. General Hillier above: no American could possibly have delivered an address like that: it is British, or Anglo–Canadian, to its very roots. The saddest thing of all is that the Canadian public know nothing of our Armed Forces, hardly recognize a Canadian military uniform when they see one, and are totally ignorant of what they are supposed to do. (Except perhaps, in an emergency, such as a flood or a forest fire or freezing rain, when they turn out in aid of the civil authorities.)

I tell you, Jean–Joseph – and above all I ask all Canadians – to look at the features of our men and women in uniform. Especially of those fine men and women who have given their lives for their country and for nobler causes. Do you not see what great looking people they are? What strong and handsome features they have, and how full of character they are!

Now look at yourself, Jean–Joseph! I cannot look at your pictures without seeing those furtive eyes, always looking askance. And look at all those wretched people – supposedly your colleagues, but in reality your yes–men, who have kept you in office and promoted your pernicious doctrines. I hold my breath as they file past: Cauchon, Caplan, Copps, Chrétien, Crapaud, Cradwanski, Colonette, Coderre, Carignan, Carolyn, Carle, Crudos, Ceaster, Crock, Cotret, Coffin and the three stooges, Callus, Callus and Callum. You are not fit to polish the boots of the least of our soldiers. Beside them you are, individually and collectively, nothing but freeloaders and pariahs, who have inflicted untold harm on Canada

Your words and deeds, and especially your words and your non–deeds, remind me constantly of this ringing statement of John Stuart Mill:

> War is an ugly thing, but not the ugliest of things; the decayed and degraded state of moral and patriotic feeling which thinks that nothing is worth war is much worse. A man who has nothing for which he is willing to fight, nothing he cares about more than his own personal safety, is a miserable creature who has no chance of being free; unless made and kept so by the exertions of better men than himself.

That is you to a tee, Jean–Joseph.

FOREIGN AFFAIRS

The three most important responsibilities of any government (after education) are those of Finance, Defence and Security, and Foreign Affairs.

During the interminable ten–year period of your prime ministership, you have not once allowed a full–scale debate on Defence Policy. And you have not allowed in all that time one single all–party debate on Foreign Affairs. Why? Because you might hear opinions that you don't want to hear, opinions that might just sway some of your otherwise servile Liberal MPs.

Defence policy, if such a thing exists in your administration, has been determined by two things: foreign policy, and your personal prejudices. (Of which more later.) Your government's foreign policy goes under the odd, and self-contradictory, name of "soft power". This policy is the handiwork of the former long-time foreign minister, Lloyd Axworthy. (Unless it was you who dictated the concept to Axworthy, who was in tune with it, and who readily promoted it and accepted authorship of it.)

We are not going to enter into a discussion of its merits and demerits, or even what it means.. Except to say this, that it eschews military action at almost all costs, and seeks peaceful solutions to every conflict between nations. (The various agencies and academic bodies that study what is called "Conflict Resolution" is mostly derisory–unless it refers to marital disagreement.) It believes that this pacifist stance will give the government and its ambassadors and negotiators great influence and leverage among nations when conflict arises.

We have seen this policy acted out on the international stage before in history. It took place in Europe in the 1930s, when fascism (Mussolini, 1922: extreme right), and nazism (Hitler, 1933: far left) threatened the peace of Europe. There were many politicians in Britain and France who were prepared to go to any lengths to avoid war, even at the cost of dishonour and humiliation. The policy was called Appeasement. The rest of the story is known: it led directly to a terrible war for which the West was unprepared, and which could have been averted by strong, resolute and timely action as early as 1936.

It is legitimate to create and to pursue an independent foreign policy. But that policy must be coherent and consistent; it must meet the needs of the times; it must make for greater security for one's country, as well as for greater amity between nations, especially like-minded nations; and it must not antagonize our traditional allies.

Your policy of "soft power" meets none of these criteria. Indeed, it endangers our security, and it has brought about a decline in our position in the world to the point where we now have no influence among our friends. It has had precisely the contrary results. It has led directly to hobnobbing with dictators, and offending our traditional allies and friends. But one must ask the serious question: Is this switch from our century-old pact of alliances with like-minded democracies to playing patsy to thugs a part of your calculated, secret agenda? Or are you just stupid, or totally indifferent to the security of Canada? The question is, perhaps, Which Canada?

I began by looking at all your ministers and government departments. Let's have another look, shall we? What do we find? We find departments of Asia–Pacific, Central & East European, Middle East, Latin America and Africa, and Francophonie. What we do not find is a department for the United States, for the European Union, or for NATO. Nor do we find a department for the Commonwealth. For you, the European Union means one thing only: France. That is a portfolio that you will handle. Canada is, or was, an influential member of the Commonwealth. No longer. You have eliminated the office. And you have replaced it by the inconsequential 'francophonie'. For obvious and unworthy reasons.

By various subtle, and not so subtle, means, you have estranged yourself from the American sphere of influence, as you have from the English–speaking world. Not only do you feel yourself thoroughly inferior in their company, in view of their dominant position in world affairs; you also feel a kinship with the other world, the so-called Third World, even if that world is largely governed by military thugs and dictators. The reasons for that switch, that kinship, are two. First, you yourself are of that mentality, as you have demonstrated by your autocratic style for the past ten years. And second, you have come under the influence of Jacques Chirac, the anti-American President of France.

Your sympathy with the political dregs on the international scene is well documented. You, like your mentor Trudeau, are pally with dictator Castro, who regularly imprisons brave men and women whose only crime is to seek some recognition of basic human rights. You have persistently espoused the cause of Arafat, the terrorist ruler of the Palestinian Authority, against Israel, the only democratic country in the Middle East. You have sided with Mugabe, the murderous dictator of Zimbabwe, against most other Commonwealth countries. And you did everything you could to weasel out of any action to topple Saddam Hussein. It is fitting to speculate on your motives for defending these thugs. Can it be because their political parties, the Zimbabwean ANU-PF, and the Ba'ath Party, are as socialist as your Liberal Party?. That will also explain more than adequately why the CBC, whose top honchos are your appointed nominees, is known as the LPC – that is, the Liberal Propaganda Party.

There is worse. You have sheltered known terrorist organizations in Canada and allowed them to collect money destined for their terrorist conspirators. You have been to conferences organized by known terrorist outfits. When you have applauded speeches by the Hezbollah leader and shaken hands with him, and when reminded who he was, you have shrugged as if, either you did not know, or, if knowing, you didn't give a damn who saw it. In either case, your conduct as the government leader of a Western democratic country is beyond contempt: it is verging on treason.

Then, of course, we have the abomination of what today is called, too simply, nine–eleven, that is, the destruction of buildings in New York City and Washington by fanatics trained and paid by Islamic terrorist groups. The United States immediately invoked the relevant article of the North Atlantic Treaty Organization, and there was an immediate, affirmative response. Then things began to fall apart. You are one of the principal agents of the anti–American camp that has betrayed the Americans.

It will forever be held against you, and become an integral part of your deplorable legacy, that on the very day after this attack, you attended a service in an Islamic mosque, where you uttered words of sympathy with the Moslem congregation. Statesmanship demanded that, in the name of all Canadians, you give them a stern reminder that they were legally and morally obliged to act as Canadians first and foremost; and the even sterner warning that anything they did as Moslems that was hostile to Canadian security would lead to their immediate expulsion from Canada. To these statements you had the duty, as the representative of all Canadians, to inform them that, if they knew of any fellow–Muslims who belonged to any terrorist organization, they had the imperative obligation to their new country to report them. When asked about border security or troop deployments or post-9/11 issues, all anyone can get out of you is :"I was proud to visit da mosques because dat to me is da Canadian values."

Your conduct in the following days, weeks and months became so outrageous that one wondered whether you had lost your mind or actually gone over to the side of the terrorists. What did you do? You gave comfort to the enemy by actually suggesting that the

Americans had brought this act of war upon their homeland upon themselves.

Some of your government members – one of them was the Caplan woman – actually insulted the President of the United States in public, at international meetings. Did you reprimand them immediately and publicly? Did you sack them on the spot? No, you totally ignored their outrageous outburst. Your very silence and lack of action branded you as an accessory. More, it indicted you as a conspirator in the camp of the anti–Americans. There is undoubtedly a strong anti–American animus in many sectors of Canadian society today. Your duty – you do not understand duty, do you? – was to face this unpleasantness head on, and combat it in the greater interest of global peace. Instead, you fed this ugly movement by your silence; you did more, you encouraged it by your subsequent words and deeds. By your very speeches you went so far as to give comfort to the enemies of all democratic institutions by siding with the terrorists and actually suggesting that the Americans were partly responsible for the attacks on their homeland. The actions and votes you have ordered in the United Nations have only served to confirm this side of your political personality, and your secret agenda. Canada's record in the United

Nations, in voting persistently on the side of Arab fascist and terrorist states and against the democratic state of Israel, serve only to add yet another nail in the coffin of your political legacy.

When it came to taking sides in the war against Iraq, you showed your true colours to the world, long though you tried to worm and weasel your way out of doing it. For months you contradicted the ministers of defence and foreign affairs; for months you seemed to take first one side then the other, but without committing yourself. Your 'final' word was to await the decision of the Security Council of the United Nations-but always with the escape-hatch that, if the UN decided on backing the Anglo-American decision to liberate the Iraqi people from its murderous régime, you would have ready your argument for not committing troops.

Your one seeming solid commitment was to the United Nations. Far from being aware that allowing the United Nations to decide Canada's foreign or other policies was a surrender of our sovereignty - a precious commodity you would never compromise! It was equally clear that your United Nations 'act' was in itself a mere pose. But the fact that Libya heads the Committee of Human Rights must have given you great confidence in the UN. For the UN, in the words of Paul Johnson, the eminent British historian is "a theatre of hypocrisy, a stink of corruption, a street market of sordid bargains and a seminary of cynicism."

One is tempted to add that that explains your attachment to the UN: you and it go hand in hand. But I know, and you know, and everyone knows, that, despite your joint affiliation, the UN is merely a skirt you hide behind. For you only adopt a UN policy or decision if it suits you. You have no hesitation in finding excuses for distancing yourself from a previous announcement if it suits your whim of the moment.

But your agents were working hard behind the scenes to avoid any unpleasant eventuality, such as providing troops for a war in Iraq. Your ambassador in Paris was, and is, none other than your own nephew, Raymond Chrétien. Your 'man in Paris' was in intimate relations with Jacques Chirac. Before this, he had been Canada's unworthy ambassador in Washington. There he had committed the typically Chrétien–like blunder of taking political sides in the presidential election by expressing a clear preference for the Democratic candidate against the Republican. This interference in the domestic politics of another, and supposedly friendly, country, which was carried out on your obvious instructions, marked you out in the eyes of the winning American President, as an enemy not only of the Republican Party of the United States, but as an enemy of the democratic process. (You have demonstrated this ugly side of your political nature by actually lobbying foreign governments to the end of freeing terrorists, on the sole ground that they were Canadian immigrants.)

Your agent in Paris concerted plans with Chirac to oppose the American resolution put before the United Nations. Of course, it was universally known that Chirac had long personal ties with Saddam Hussain, the unspeakable butcher of Iraq, and had investments in the Iraq oil industry worth at least forty billion dollars. Chirac did not want to lose that investment, and put every obstacle possible in the way of a successful UN resolution. And you supported him. (What was your reward for your services? Chirac, of course, as is well known, is a so–far–unconvicted crook. As mayor of Paris for 18 years he is suspected of engaging in all sorts of dirty tricks, and would have been indicted had he not become President and managed to invoke a law that precluded the indictment of a sitting President. Let us hope that the justices of France have a long memory.) It is scarcely surprising that such a ruler would appeal to you, eh, Jean-Joseph?

I have said that it is legitimate for any country to have an independent foreign policy. For Canada to embark on a foreign policy not only at odds with its ancient allies, but actually hostile to them, is a move unprecedented in Canadian history since 1812. But that is what you have done. Foreign relations and foreign policies are most successful when based on firm personal relations between heads of government. You know that perfectly well. It was your primary duty to pursue a good personal relationship with President Bush. Had you done that from the beginning, it would have been possible for you to explain your opposition to the Iraq war, and still retain his respect. You must have known that by your subterfuge and evasion, and your countenancing of the anti-American expressions mouthed by many of your fellow-Liberals, you were courting a backlash on the part of the US Government. The measures they took against our softwood lumber, our wheat, and our beef, to mention only three exported commodities, you knew would inflict severe economic hardship on important sectors of Canadian trade. Be it noted, however, that it was trade of Western Canada that was affected, and for that you didn't give a damn, and have taken no visible steps to correct.

But you didn't establish good relations with President Bush: you were filled with hatred of him, and succumbed to the temptation of letting your personal feelings overpower your feeble reason and to dictate national policy. Whose side are you on: George Bush or Saddam Hussein? Whose side is Chirac on – Bush or Saddam Hussein? Your final decision makes it clear beyond all doubt that you tend to side with the oppressor and the dictator, rather than with the forces of democracy unless forced.

The three overarching requirements of foreign policy are:
1) Security
2) Prosperity
3) Inter-dependence.
No country, no matter how powerful, can exist in a vacuum. "No man is an island." No nation either. All peoples need allies and friends and partners. The weaker a country is, the more exigent is the need for allies. No nation can achieve total sovereignty either. Every pact, alliance and dependence – that is, security and

prosperity – are only realized at the expense of elements of one's sovereignty. But let it be understood with crystal clarity that the surrender of every parcel of one's national sovereignty is made willingly in the interest of a greater gain. Provided – and let us repeat this primordial principle of foreign policy – provided that it is accompanied by an equal gain in the security and prosperity of the like-minded nations one forms alliances and partnerships with. Let us know who our friends are, who is hostile to us, and who are neither and who might switch back and forth.

The security and prosperity of a people and nation can only be achieved by defence and trade policies which serve two mutually rewarding ends: the security and prosperity of ourselves, and the security and prosperity of our partners and allies.

In ten years you have issued only one White Paper on foreign policy. It was a mish–mash of pious pontificating about values – not even Canadian values at that – and void of any discussion of our strategic and global interests.

Since then, earlier this year, the impotent Foreign Minister, Bill Graham, has issued a paper which enlarges on the 'values' theme and ignores the only authentic concerns of an independent and sovereign nation. "Canada's foreign policy agenda (he has written, or approved) must reflect the nation we are: a multicultural, bilingual society that is free, open, prosperous and democratic. The experiences of immigrants from around the world and the cultures of our Aboriginal peoples are woven into the fabric of our national identity. Respect for equality and diversity runs through the religious, racial, cultural and linguistic strands forming our communities."

That is an accurate summary of the Liberal dogma as might be regurgitated in any essay submitted by a freshman student in Sociology 101– though even the free, open and democratic 'values' are subject to question.. What it has to do with foreign policy is beyond imagining. One readily pictures the scribes in the Prime Minister's Office burning the midnight oil night after night in their windowless towers, striving to compose a stirring 'agenda' that would pull a few more layers of wool over the minister's eyes, and indifferent to the charge that it was lifted from Jean–Joseph's Gospel of Political Correctness.

The evidence of your ten-year misgovernment, Jean-Joseph, shows a persistent ignorance of or indifference to the fundamental interests and needs of Canada.

One cannot conclude a discussion of foreign policy without addressing the vital, and intimately related, question of our policy with respect to immigrants and refugees. No examination of the record of your administration can but conclude that you have taken steps to exclude people from Western Europe and the English-speaking countries, and to admit as many as possible from other countries, especially from the so-called third world countries. In the past, rigorous standards of health, education and cultural fitness were applied. You, on the other hand, have preferred to welcome almost anyone from the impoverished countries, whether they had any skills or not to offer to Canada, and whether they had any connection with contagious diseases or with terrorist organizations.

And the corruption within the immigration departments of some overseas embassies, where local personnel are hired without a security check, and then employed to issue visas to emigrate to Canada, is of a piece with the moral status of your administration almost since Day One of your premiership.

SUMMING UP

You, M. Chrétien, are a politician. You have been a politician for 40 years. In fact, this month of October, you will have been a politician for exactly 40 years. In the course of those 40 years you will have acquired very considerable political skills. Now, one is tempted to ask: What are those political skills? And, even more to the point, what have you used them for?

Before I launch into an examination of those questions, I will quietly remind you – and the public – that last year you 'persuaded' Herb Grey to resign his seat. Why was that? It was, quite simply, because Mr. Grey, who was one of the most honourable and respected Members, was approaching his 40th anniversary as a Member of Parliament, and you didn't want him to get there before you. Or to get there at all, especially when your 40th anniversary was coming up. You, Jean–Joseph Chrétien, exhibited some of the salient features of your character, namely, pettiness, jealousy, and vindictiveness.

So, you are a politician. It is probably a badge you would be proud to wear, in the light of your many electoral victories at the polls. But, as you will unquestionably recognize, though never admit to, politics is a dirty business. And you are skilled in the political business. After all, didn't you used to boast of being a "street fighter"? Though you wouldn't admit to it today, when you find yourself on the eve of your retirement from an active role in Canadian politics. And hoping, it is reported, of becoming the next Secretary General of the United Nations. God Forbid! You would be the worst ever, among a group of dismal failures, as you have proved yourself to be the worst of all Prime Ministers of Canada.

What role can a man or woman elected to Parliament play, who aspires to Machiavelli!

I wonder often whether you ever went to university. I believe you were once a practising lawyer. I am easily led to believe that you saw little future for yourself in law because you were so obviously out-distanced intellectually by the men and women you saw around you. In wiles, no, but in intellectual vigour, yes. You looked around you and what did you see? Why, you saw a potential career in politics. Why in politics? Because in politics one can get ahead by sheer bluster and graft and deviousness. And perhaps make a fortune as well.

If you went to university, you may have taken a course or two in political philosophy. Or rather in what is called, in order to avoid the notion of ethics, political science. Today, as in your day, the courses that the departments of Political Science push most energetically are those that accord best with their departmental 'philosophy'. The courses they push are those that promote the ideas of Plato, Machiavelli, Rousseau, Hegel, Marx and Lenin. I once asked a professor of political science why our universities promoted those thinkers. His answer was: "Because they are the most influential in Western history." The "most influential"? In Western history? The man was a left-wing historian. What he meant was: "the most influential in Western left thinking."

The truth is, of course–and we know: yes, we know don't we, Jean–Joseph?- that the Left is not the slightest bit interested in the truth. The Left is interested only in, and engaged only in, their agenda of propagating the ideology of the Left. This 'mission' of theirs, and of yours, is destructive of the ideals of the Western intellectual and moral traditions.

The truth of the matter – the truth of history – is that the Western tradition and Western thought have been progressing slowly, yet remorselessly, since the Renaissance, away from the intellectual shackles of the clerical Middle Ages toward a Civilization that recognizes the central importance of the individual and his place in the comity of national affairs. It was a tectonic shift away from the ecclesiastical to the rational, from the autocratic to the national, from the superstitious to the scientific – from, in a word, the arbitrary and decreed to the moral and the emancipated. No word more aptly sums up this shift than the advice given by Pantagruel to a friend who was wracked with doubt: "Are you not assured within yourself of what you have a mind to? The chief and main point of the whole matter lies therein." It was almost revolutionary in its implications, namely that a man should decide for himself what he should do. And, let us not doubt it, to accept the responsibility for the consequences of his decisions and acts.

Western thought has been fertilized by other writers, writers ignored by our left–leaning universities. They do not teach Aristotle as they should, in the place of Plato, who would have banned poets from his Republic. They carefully avoid Cicero, with his moral lessons for mankind. Machiavelli is countered by Erasmus and his *Education of a Christian Prince*, which few professors of politics have read. In the place of Rousseau we would prefer Montesquieu – and some chapters from Voltaire – and certainly Hume and Locke and Frederick's *Anti-Machiavel*. And who put in the place of people like Marx and Lenin but Burke and Paine, intellectual and political opposites though they were. Then why study them? For two reasons: 1) that it is an education in itself to put oneself into contact with great minds. (It only becomes an educational experience to encounter minds like yours if held up as horrible examples.) 2) that, as the French knew: *Du choc des opinions jaillit la lumière.* (Yes, on the condition of having a free press and free discussion.) And finally, in the 20th century, who is going to sit at the feet of Hitler and Stalin and their apologists when we have Roosevelt and Churchill and Truman? And the sage writings of Camus and Muggeridge and Orwell and Sakharov and Solzhenitsyn and Pavel – and the legion of unsung and unknown writers of the Russian *samizdat*, who risked their lives in order to keep alive the sparks of their cultural heritage and their power of freedom of thought.

Of all that, Jean–Joseph, you are totally ignorant. Or what is worse, and far more likely, while knowing something about it, you are totally indifferent, or hostile. For the fact is that your words and deeds proclaim you to be politically, intellectually and morally in harmony with the oppressors rather than in sympathy with the oppressed.

The history of political thought I have just adumbrated for you is the history of the movement from an autocratic theocracy toward a popular democracy. This is not the place to trace the evolution from monarchy to parliamentary democracy, with the concomitant birth and growth of the two factions, Tory and Whig. In Canadian political development we find, at the outset, Conservative and Liberal. There then sprung up a third faction, called either socialist or labour, as a result of the failure of the two traditional parties to address the growing social problems of an increasingly urban class of workers. The Right distrusted the Left, and the Left distrusted the Right. And so it was that the Liberal Party became the central focal point, the necessary compromise, which promised equitable dealings for all Canadians.

I will jump the gap and conclude by saying that you, Jean–Joseph Chrétien, having been elected leader of the Liberal Party of Canada in 1993 by a collection of delegates incapable of the minimum powers of discrimination essential to the choosing of a national leader – delegates who couldn't tell Joe from Jeeze – went on to subvert the traditional and honourable legacy and principles of Canadian liberalism.

The liberal tradition is compounded of a set of principles and beliefs that tend toward constitutional change and legal and other reforms that, in their turn, aim to foster freedom and democratic institutions. The bedrock of that tradition is a faith in the individual who, being free, is capable of directing his own life and making his own choices with the minimum of regulation and interference from government.

Far from honouring this tradition, you are its enemy. You engaged cheerfully on a course to corrupt our hallowed system of parliamentary democracy. You have bribed and browbeaten the people you chose to be ministers of the Crown, so that they licked your boots and never insisted that Cabinet decide all-important issues of public policy, and not by your unilateral ukase – often enough delivered by your Prime Minister's Office. You arranged things so that important matters of public policy were never debated in the House. You ensured that, if a debate could not be avoided, you enforced closure of debate in order to avoid embarrassing discussion and exposure of your threadbare ideas and to keep the caucus subservient.

Between 1913 and 1979, closure was invoked a mere 13 times. Since then, since 1980, closure – that is, the gag on freedom of debate – has been imposed on Parliament no fewer than 166 times How many of those do you take credit for?

Frequently you have brought in a motion the effect of which was to muzzle the citizens of Canada by criminalizing any expenditure of private funds aimed at the publicizing of hostility to your policies and practices during elections. (It is a dirty blot on the record of all political parties, except for the Opposition party, that they voted in favour of your motion hostile to free speech.)

You are against freedom. You are all in favour of rights. Freedom is indivisible; rights are easily manufactured, and then enacted into law by Parliament. And so subversively that the enacted rights can then be decreed by various Courts as taking precedence over our ancient freedoms.

You and the late Pierre–Elliot Trudeau are the joint authors of the Canadian Charter of Rights and Freedoms. This document is a carefully, and cunningly, contrived weapon designed to enhance 'rights' at the expense of our ancient freedoms. This document, which has subsequently shown itself to be a charter of suppression of our freedoms, has been the instrument of the promotion of policies that are proving to be destructive of Canadian unity, and of furthering Canadian disintegration.

We had no need of a Charter of Rights and Freedoms. We already had one. Indeed, we have two. They are called: *The Universal Declaration of Human Rights*, and the *International Covenant on Civil and Political Rights*. These documents are charters of the United Nations. You, Jean–Joseph, who adore the United Nations, and who side with the UN whenever an anti–Israel motion reaches the floor of the General Assembly, should be among the first to adopt these United Nations declarations. Why didn't you? Ah, but you're a politician! A politician before anything else, a man obsessed with power before anything else. A man totally indifferent to right and good and justice. And what is there in these UN charters that frightens you, and that frightened your mentor Trudeau? Why, nothing other than its articles which enshrine the right of freedom of association, and the right to the enjoyment of private property. Just think of the consequences of enacting these fundamental rights into Canadian law. Why, to mention just one unfortunate consequence, you would not be able to force employees to join trades unions, and trades unions wouldn't be able to confiscate dues from non–member employees.

The policies, which you, like, a circus barker, tout as representing Canadian values are: multiculturalism, bilingualism, appeasement, equality, rights, and political correctness. But they are far from being Canadian values: they are at the heart of your partisan Liberal values.

I will resist the delightful opportunity to analyse and dissect these subversive doctrines, other than to say, in the following summary, that they all tend, and are seemingly meant to tend, toward the disruption of Canadian unity.

Canadian unity – ah, that condition did exist until quite recent times. I would say that Canadian youngsters throughout the 1930s and '40s and '50s, and perhaps even into the '60s, all followed the same pattern of beliefs and values. If you had asked anyone – in family, community, school, church, police, or country – about right and wrong, good and bad, just and unjust, almost all would have had the same answers. Today, anything goes. Why? We may ask one of two questions. Either (1) What happened to cause the change? Or (2) Where did we go wrong? The politician, or the academic social 'scientist', will seek to answer the first question. The Canadian citizen will zero in on the second question. Why? Because the problem, and the answer, is of an inherently moral nature.

The explanation of this Canadian disunity is to be found in the Liberal policies introduced above.

Multiculturalism is a policy designed to encourage foreign immigrants to practice their native religions and cultures, at the expense of becoming Canadians first. (It is to be noted that European and other immigrants did their best to integrate themselves into Canadian society, and succeeded. For Government to invert a successful policy and practice raises the questions of intent and motive.)

Who is the minister responsible for this policy? When has she, or he, ever explained to the Canadian people what this policy entails, and its racial consequences? It is one of those insidious, and socially destructive policies, which constitute such a large part of your Liberal agenda.

In the 1930s, '40s, and even '50s, as I have said, all young Canadians lived by the same beliefs. More than that: the individual, whether a schoolchild or a parent or a teacher, was in tune with the *mores* of society as a whole. All were imbued with the same set of fundamental beliefs and values. All were Canadians first. Anything else they chose to be came second or third. Things are different today. Not only in Canada: throughout the countries and peoples that include themselves in Western Civilization, the story is the same. Civilization is going to pot. The reason is that Western pseudo-philosophers, and even churchmen, have been spreading the satanic doctrine that Man is not a moral being, and not therefore subject to moral laws. And how you politicians lap it up!

The sad thing, Jean–Joseph, is that you, the avowed Catholic, seem to have embraced this perverse and destructive doctrine because it accords with your political methods and aims. The statesman would confront the situation and devise policies to promote national and social unity. You have followed the opposite path.

No country will ever amount to anything whose people do not form one homogeneous whole, embracing the same values and social principles, and living by the same customs. But no: you do not want immigrants to be assimilated into the population, which is English-speaking. If they do, they will inter-marry. God forbid! They could end up voting Conservative or New Democratic – or even worse, Canadian Alliance! No: you want them to remain as Sikhs and Hindus and Muslims, as Tamils and Vietnamese and Koreans and Thais. That way, living apart with their customs and practices actually encouraged and funded by the Ottawa, they will continue to vote Liberal. What if it had happened in, say, Alberta? Why, you would have imposed the Supreme Court's ruling. And why? Because few people in Alberta vote Liberal.

Bilingualism was, at the outset, a worthy social aim, as created by the late Lester B. Pearson, who saw in it a bridge to cross the wide gap between Quebec and Anglo-Canadian cultures, values, and interests. The great mistake of its authors was to try to plant it in the English schools. The mistake was twofold. First, the idea that the ability to speak a second language would necessarily lead to an understanding by the learners of the people whose language they were learning. It just isn't so. The second, and worse, error was to cause the schools to embark on a programme of language teaching that was to emphasize the spoken word to the detriment of the written word. The ability to speak a foreign language is no evidence of education. Millions of people throughout the world speak several languages, but cannot read and write. In a word, the education of millions of our children was debased for political ends. There is not an iota of evidence to show that Canada is any closer to unity, or that Quebec is any further from independence, because of the policy of bilingualism.

The other side of the bilingualism policy is even uglier. Within the secret and tortuous corridors of government offices and ministries, the word has been passed that 'bilingualism' meant one thing only. It meant, and means to this day: a bilingual person is a person whose mother tongue is French, and who has a basic knowledge of spoken English. A person whose mother tongue is any language other than

French, no matter how fluent in French that person may be, can only be considered for employment in a position classified as "a bilingual position" after every properly bilingual applicant has been considered. This bigoted policy is in force not only in the Civil Service, but also in the traditionally 'English' institutions such as the RCMP and the Armed Forces – at a very great cost to professional efficiency and morale. If the CBC can comprise two separate entities – English and French – there is no good reason why the RCMP and the Armed Forces cannot be organized in the same practical way. No good reason. Only a disruptive political reason.

Several years ago the Quebec Government enacted a language law that relegated English in Quebec to an inferior status, in commerce, in education, etc. etc. An appeal to the Supreme Court was upheld, and the law declared unconstitutional. What did you do, Jean Chrétien? You did nothing. You did not enforce the decision of the Supreme Court of Canada. Why not? Why, because you would lose votes. How legally and morally disgusting a prime minister can get! But then, of course, you are not a Canadian, you are a Quebecker. You have always been a Quebecker; you have never been a Canadian, no matter how much you spout about "da Canadian valews". The theme and mentions of Canada in your utterances have been for Anglo consumption only. Quebeckers have never for one moment been hoodwinked. That is why the separatist movement is as strong today as it was when you became prime minister ten years ago.

Appeasement. Appeasement is the name I give to your permanent, unwritten policy of buying people and groups off. It is a form of bribery. It has been your practice ever since you have been in politics. Appeasement, as you practice it, has two forms. Firstly, it is the practice of spending vast sums of public moneys, both to Liberal ridings to ensure their future 'loyalty', and, above all, to Quebec to buy their adherence to the federal system. I avoided saying 'adherence to Canada' because about 40% of the Quebec people are not interested in Canada, except in so far as they can continue to feed from the milch cow.

Stop Press! As I write, at the end of October, there appears in the independent newspapers the further scandal – amid a host of scandals relating to several ministers accepting hand-outs and favours from a wealthy capitalist who expects contracts in return, and then scurrying into denial or justification – the further scandal, I say, of your Minister responsible for the Atlantic Canada Opportunities Agency, a nobody named Gerry Byrne, funnelling over half of the millions earmarked for fishermen (fishermen thrown out of work by your Atlantic fishery policies) into his own constituency. His reaction when accused of unethical conduct? Excuses, justifications, excuses! Well, what's so odd about it? It is, after all, a well-established Liberal practice, of which you are the chief exponent!

<u>Stop Press!</u>   Another scandal. You, Jean-Joseph, authorized the spending of over five million dollars on a small private airport in Quebec, with very limited traffic, and open only for six months of the year. Other small airports in different parts of Canada, with much heavier traffic, and open year round, were denied moneys or got only a small fraction of what they needed and applied for. The reasons? The airports that went unfunded were in constituencies that did not have Liberal MPs, or were in Western Canada; and the over-funded airport was close to the private estate of one Paul Desmarais. Who is Paul Desmarais? Why, he is the father of the fellow your daughter France married! How cosy! How convenient! How utterly corrupt. There is more. This Desmarais imported vast quantities of vintage

wines for lavish parties held for over 200 people, and never had to pay a nickel of duty. How cosy! How convenient! How utterly corrupt.

The other facet of what I call 'appeasement' has to do with ingratiating yourself – yes, you personally, and degradingly – with large segments of immigrants to Canada. This unseemly practice of yours has been greatly in evidence since the terrorist attacks on the United States. You have gone out of your way to be unctuous toward Muslims and Sikhs and Palestinians, among others. There seems to be a particularly jelly–like component of your backbone that is terrified of giving offence, or even of seeming to give offence, to this segment of our immigrant population, even of those who are not yet Canadians. Yet you hesitate not a second to give offence to our Jewish compatriots and to the brave people of Israel. Does the explanation lie solely in your calculation of votes to be gained for your party? Or are you a racist? Or perhaps – which is the same thing – you are so thoroughly anti–American and anti–English that you will go to any lengths to show it?

Equality. Equality is one of those terms that have an immediate appeal as stemming from our yearning for fairness and justice in dealing with the problems and difficulties of life.

We know, from experience, often bitter, that things are not equal, and that any intervention that can help to make things even a little less unequal is to be welcomed, as a step forward in our striving for a civilized life.

People are not equal, as we know, in physical abilities such as strength and endurance. People are not equal in their talents and mental equipment. Indeed, it might be argued that a world in which all people were equal would be intolerably dull. Not only that, but the very fact of all being equal would for ever prevent any sort of improvement or progress in any human endeavour.

Just as we yearn for fairness, we also positively desire and need inequality. We want to excel, and do better than others. We want our team to beat the opponents. Yes, but let us add: fairly, not by any means. I will further, and say: we want our opponents to excel, to surpass themselves, so that we can claim a worthy result, and be tested to the limit.

Where we insist on absolute equality – if any kind of absolute can exist – is in law. And that is all that our striving for equality should mean. We must all be held as equal before the law; all must play on the same level playing field; there must be no favouritism, no bias or prejudice, in the dealings of the legally constituted authorities with all citizens. For the rest, we are free to exercise and exploit our natural and acquired abilities to further our ambitions and aims.

Where inequality is offensive is in the power and willingness of the authorities to enrich themselves and their friends, to allocate special favours and 'perks' to themselves and their associates, at the expense of the public purse. We all know the famous passage in George Orwell's *Animal Farm* where the pigs, who have seized control of the farm and instituted a regime where all are equal, declare that, "Some pigs are more equal than others." Does that ring a bell, Jean-Joseph?

There is, however, another manifestation of official equality, which is not only offensive: it tends to undermine the foundations of human society. It is the policy of your government to act on the assumption, never demonstrated, that all policies, all regulations, and especially all rights are exactly equal in worth. This is a monstrous premise on which to base decisions of government and relations with the public. Rights and policies are not equal. It is only for people of no integrity, and lacking in principle, that these things are deemed equal, for to say otherwise is to require choices, which means to establish priorities, and choice assumes a certain liberty in the matter, and the exercise of liberty is only possible for a moral person.

Rights. Rights means human rights. (To suggest that animals have rights, as some people claim, is to turn rights on its head and to make nonsense of it. What they mean, presumably, is that humans have certain responsibilities toward animals, be they domestic – household or farm – or wild. Let them say so, and act accordingly.)

Rights not only means human rights: it means, essentially, basic human rights. Or, even better, imprescriptible rights. Morally – and legally too, if our society were governed rightfully – rights are twinned with responsibilities. There is no right that can be exercised in isolation from one's duties as a citizen. We are all part and parcel of a larger whole. The larger whole confers on us certain rights; we in our turn must make a return of some kind. Ingrained selfishness is the most abject of human defects – worse even than fleeing in the face of the enemy. What we return for the gift of the rights we receive must be determined by each individual. They cannot be legislated.

Canada today has become a culture of rights. Every Tom, Dick and Harry demands his rights! What rights? He demands the right – that is, the freedom: no, worse, the licence – to do what the hell he pleases. And more often than not he is supported by your government, which has set up an intrusive system of Human Rights Commissions throughout the land, the whole purpose of which is to champion the so-called rights of the least deserving members of our society against the law-abiding, tax-paying majority. What rights?

- The right of anyone to lie on the sidewalks of our cities with their underfed dogs and demand money from passers-by and obstruct their passing.
- The right of druggies to get free needles to indulge their vice.
- The right of 12-year old girls to leave their families and to shack up with boys scarcely older than them.
- The right of children to leave their homes, to set up on their own, and to be supported by their parents.

- ♉ The right of mere children to consult doctors and to have their records kept secret from their parents.
- ♉ The right of convicted criminals to enjoy – get this! – conjugal rights.
- ♉ The right of convicted criminals to have colour TVs in their cells.
- ♉ The right of convicted criminals to vote in federal elections. (Note: One supposes that their vote will automatically be cast in favour of you Liberals. This 'right' was granted by judges of the Supreme Court of Canada, most of whom were appointed by you, the Great Magistrate.)
- ♉ The right of known war criminals in Canada to be set free by your anti-Canadian Immigration minister, one Coderre, and their right to privacy which prevents the same Coderre from making public their names and photographs.
- ♉ The rights of foreign terrorists to enter Canada without a background check and to set up cells for future infiltration into the United States.
- ♉ The right of professional unionists, such as teachers and civil servants and airline pilots, to go on strike.
- ♉ The right of married women to undergo an abortion without the consent of their husbands.

- ୪ The right of homosexuals to stage a parade in any Canadian city contrary to the express wish of the city council.

- ୪ The right of a Human Rights Commission, appointed – not elected – by one of your satraps to order a city mayor to issue a permit to a homosexual group to organize a public parade.

- ୪ The right of any female to make an accusation of sexual harassment against any male person, with the sure knowledge that her accusation will be accepted as gospel, without due process, even in universities whose charters enjoin the fundamental moral duty of seeking truth above all.

- ୪ The right of people to eat and drink in our streets and other public places, and to leave their garbage lying about.

- ୪ The right of house owners to make an infernal racket with their leaf–blowers in residential neighbourhoods on Saturday evenings and Sundays.

- ୪ The right of yahoos to drive round our cities and towns with their windows open and with their CD players blaring at full blast.

- ୪ The right of other yahoos to go screaming around lakes with their sea–doos, endangering swimmers and water skiers and fishermen.

The list can go on and on. But we will conclude with the worst one of all the above, bad though they are:

- ♉ The right of the Prime Minister to appoint as judges, ambassadors, and heads of Crown corporations at vast salaries, people who have demonstrated no or inadequate aptitude or capacity for their appointments.

It is absolutely critical to distinguish freedoms from rights. Freedoms are not rights. Do not believe people who talk about the 'right to freely express your views'. The distinction is this: Freedoms are not granted by government or any other authority, except in totalitarian states. Where, of course, freedoms are non-existent. And you, Jean–Joseph, are the first among Liberals to appreciate that. Freedoms are an inherent possession of all free people. It is the ultimate and most prized dream of all slave peoples. Authorities – and I include you, Jean–Joseph – are all too keen to abrogate to themselves the power to decide what rights and freedoms that we, the citizens, shall have. For the simple reason that, once we accept that claim, we have surrendered our freedom. If we once accept that government can grant freedom, they can take it away. Do not fall for it! More than that. I say to you all, to all Canadians who believe yourselves to be free, to ask yourselves this question: At what point in the evolving history of our nation and people are you prepared to revolt against the constituted authority? And let there be no mistake about it: by revolt I mean to assemble arms en masse and to storm the seat of government. Any people who are not prepared to do that at some critical juncture in their history are not worth fighting for.

Political Correctness. As for this pillar of your agenda, all we need to say for the moment is that it is a duplicitous stratagem, greeted initially with ridicule, but too late recognized for what it is, a subterfuge designed to stifle freedom of expression. It has so far achieved its objectives as to silence even professors in their protected enclaves of privilege. But then, who ever expected anything of our professors but people who professed nothing, who taught no philosophy, who had mastered no arts, and who (with a tiny few admirable exceptions) were abject cowards – on the model of your fellow Cabinet ministers, who, equally without principle, are gung–ho on receiving their daily rewards for the mere act of kissing the feet of their paymasters.

BROKEN PROMISES

At the slight risk of repetition I am going to append a list of some of your uncountable sins of commission. By that I mean all the promises you made back in 1993 with the intent of persuading the public, when seeking political office, both of your political agenda and of your seriousness and honesty of purpose.

I hope that you will shiver at the sight of these broken promises, but I am quite sure you will not, and that for two reasons: one, you are devoid of any sense of shame, as you are of moral principle; and two, you have no more elections to contest and hence no more voters to court and bribe.

Your famous – no, make that infamous – Red Book promised:
- To abolish the GST
- To renegotiate the NAFTA
- To enact a Code of Conduct for Members of Parliament
- To appoint very senior officials on the basis of competence
- To allow many free votes in the House

♉ To do away with trade barriers within Canada

The list goes on and on. To it we will add the cancellation of the helicopter contract signed by the previous Government, the cancellation of which cost us, the taxpayers, eight hundred million dollars. And the cancellation of the Pearson Airport contract, which cost us taxpayers a further several hundred millions of dollars.

To it I will also repeat your promise to appoint an Ethics Counsellor who would report directly to Parliament, and not to you as Prime Minister. The idea of you, Jean–Joseph, setting yourself up as the arbiter of right and wrong is as hilarious as it would be to ask the two ugly Robinson sisters, Gene and Sbent, to aid in the drawing up a statement on holy matrimony! Or to expect Kofi Annan to condemn the atrocities perpetrated by Arafat! Or to see Maurice Strong or David Suzuki attack the Kyoto Agreement, discredited as it is! Or, heaven forfend! to ask Maude Barlow to chair a meeting dedicated to the advancement of global free trade.

Come to think of it, why is this Barlow woman and her Council of Canadians – and I put this question to you, Jean–Joseph – why are Barlow and umpteen other NGOs (Non-Government Organizations) subsidized to the tune of tens of millions of taxpayers' dollars every year to carry out their agendas of undermining and opposing the very structures of the economic and political foundations of Canada? You have a helluva lot of explaining to do. But you will never get around to the explaining you have to do because you are a master of evading your responsibilities and the motives of your actions and inactions.

Mais quoi! An ethics counsellor is assuredly the most pressing and vital requirement for your Government today, for you and your fellow back-slappers have shown that you do not know the difference between right and wrong. And often Canadians wonder whether you care, so keen are you all on acquiring power and wealth.

I come now to the penultimate article of this zolean J'accuse!

You, Jean-Joseph, are a practised politician. The keenest insight of the practised politician, of the politician who, like you, is unencumbered by principles, is his ability to discern the weaknesses of his opponents, who are hedged in by principles.

The question boils down to this: Are we a free people? Or are we a weak people who need to be managed, controlled, regulated, and directed?

It is the saddest thing in the world for a Canadian – for a Canadian who believes that Canada is capable of things greater than she has ever achieved in the past, both on the national scene and in the international arena – to have to admit that we have become a servile Nanny State. It is to the eternal discredit and shame of the Liberal Party of Canada, aided and abetted by the socialist New Democratic Party, that you, as its head, have betrayed all the traditional principles of Liberalism, and spent all your energies on reducing Canadians to a servile dependence on government.

Canadians of all stripes have come to believe that government is good, and works for the good and the welfare of all Canadians. The record of your administration, like the evidence of your words and deeds – as of all that you have failed to do and to say – proves the contrary. Your sole political purpose has been to satisfy your obsession with control and direction. The very idea that such a corrupt person as you should be in a position to influence and direct the lives of people who are by far your superiors is almost enough to make one despair of democracy in Canada.

A second facet of this same theme is the readiness of individuals to run to some authority or other to solve their personal problems. Every day the press – the term 'media' is ridiculous – is filled with tales of individuals who have been offended in some way or another. They have been encouraged to scurry to the nearest authority person to seek protection or redress. The authorities have been conditioned by the repulsive doctrine of political correctness to give credence to any accusation of 'wrong-doing' by, say, a faculty member or a student. The dean, or other authority, immediately accepts the accusation, and unleashes a process of hearings. In a word, he (or she) throws overboard all idea of due process, and defiles the sacrosanct principle of innocence until convicted.

Canada's existence as a free and democratic country is founded on the principle of the rule of law. The rule of law is one of the very greatest inventions of the human mind. Indispensable to this principle is the doctrine of personal responsibility. But what do we find today? The very opposite! You, Jean–Joseph, are perverting the powers of the State when you support individuals who sue corporations for having supposedly caused any medical or other problems. I mean, how can a tobacco company be responsible for the addiction to their product of a kid who starts smoking under the pressure of his peers?

Can a coffee shop be held responsible for the scalding of a customer who drives off in her car with a cup of hot coffee held between her knees? Can a host be held criminally or civilly responsible for any harm done by a guest – especially an uninvited guest – who gets drunk and, despite pleas by the host and other guests, drives off and kills some unfortunate cyclist?

What next? Will a builder be held accountable for the injuries of a person who falls down the stairs of his house? And yet all these cases, and many more, have been brought before our courts.

The fact that people today seek to avoid their personal responsibility for mishaps or worse can be laid at your feet. For you, Jean–Joseph, are the greatest evader of responsibility of all Canadians. You personally, and your fellow Cabinet ministers, are in a constant state of denial when evidence of your wrongdoing in many of its forms is made public.

If you had been in business or finance you would have been arraigned many years ago for abuse of public funds. If you had been in law, one hopes you would have been expelled for unethical conduct. If you had been in a university position, one would have sought your discharge for moral turpitude. And if you had been in the Church you would have been excommunicated – as in fact you should be today for your thumb–in–the–nose attitude toward the Pope.

You are not in business or law or academe or the Church. You are in politics. And for you, in politics anything goes. Earlier I talked about responsibility and leadership. You have signally demonstrated your incapacity for leadership, since you have constantly demonstrated your refusal of responsibility.

Many opportunities have arisen for you to demonstrate leadership. You have signally shown your incapacity. I think of the floods in Manitoba. You turned up only after weeks of biting criticism in the daily press, and then only for twenty minutes, to stage what is called by the cynical press a photo–op, showing you handing a sandbag to a weary worker. On the second anniversary of the attack on the World Trade Center, you issued a flaccid statement from your heavily subsidized riding of Shawinigan. As one Canadian journalist wrote: "He just doesn't care. Or he just doesn't get it." (I suggest it's far worse than that.) Where were you when the World Health Organization issued a travel advisory against visiting Toronto because of SARS? You were sunning yourself at a Caribbean resort (at whose expense?), and you had no intention of returning to deal with it.

The devastating forest fires in the Okanagan of British Columbia last summer did not concern you in the least – until a similar barrage of critical condemnation finally aroused your 'handlers' or 'agents' or 'aides' to persuade you at least put in an appearance. And what did you do? Why, they actually got you into a helicopter to fly you over a line very distant from the fire itself, to the acclaim of Liberal trumpets, and very little press coverage.

Where were you when Ontario and much of New England were blacked out by a huge power failure? Why, you were safe in your constituency, unheeding of the crisis, because you had all the electricity you needed.

The interesting thing is that while you were avoiding the power crisis that was going on down south, your pal Jacques Chirac, the President of France, was absent from Paris. And what was going on in France at the time? Well, as it happens, he was taking a leaf out of your book by staying as far from trouble as possible while thousands of his fellow countrymen were dying in the heat wave that was frying most of Europe. (The death toll in France was worse than in other European countries for the reason that the French are the most unneighbourly people in the world. No one knows his neighbour, and cares less. Of course, you, Jean-Joseph, are French to the core!) But if Chirac was not in France at the time, while his compatriots died in the thousands, where was he? Why, he was on holiday in Quebec, near Shawinigan of all places! What a strange coincidence! The thing that intrigues Canadians, however, is, why you were holed up together at this time, when there were crises in both their countries. You must surely have been brought together for State matters of much greater importance than a mere heat wave – even the worst heat wave in Europe for 400 years – or than an epidemic or forest fires?

Well, of course! Chirac was pressuring you to side with him, in the United Nations and elsewhere, against the Americans over the Iraq business. You see – if you didn't know before, which we all believe – Chirac made it perfectly clear that he had entered into personal contracts with Saddam Hussein to the tune of about forty billions of dollars over oil construction and supplies, and he was mighty keen to get you onside in any future international dispute over that investment. For he was only too aware of the international law called "dettes odieuses", which voids debts such as Saddam's to Chirac's France.

What else did you and your arch–villain pal discuss? Souring relations with the United States, *la francophonie* vs. the Commonwealth, increasing trade, Quebec autonomy and nationhood, the merits of Islam, bla, bla, bla. I feel sure that a tape of your discussions would shake the world even of a naive Axworthian diplomacy. But for the fact that it is almost certain that other intelligence agencies were more than aware of your little get–together and would have contrived access to your most private discussions. Hey, Jean! I suggest you check your clothing for those tiny little bugs! You did? Well, I'm not sure you can count on CSIS! Did you not know that you are the suspect?

You have demonstrated beyond all cavil and contest that you have used all the means you control to suppress or limit the most sacred freedoms that have existed in Canada for over one hundred years, and for which thousands of Canadians have given their lives in wars in defence of our cherished liberties. If there is one item in your legacy that will forever stamp you as a villain of the most egregious kind, it is your constant efforts to substitute your Liberal 'rights' for Canadians' legitimate freedoms.

In your quest to subvert the very legal and moral foundations of Parliament, and hence of Canada, you have appointed judges to the Supreme Court of Canada who have carried out your secret agenda of smothering our sacred and imprescriptible freedoms under a legalistic heap of manufactured rights. Right-thinking Canadians will never forget, and never forgive, that woman Justice who, when an appellant cited the New Testament as evidence of Christian condemnation of the male homosexual practice while loving the sinner, questioned sneeringly: "What's all this love stuff?" In so sneering, she was declaring open war against the very heart of Christian ethics. And, yes, the very soul of the ethical principles that have sustained Canada for well over two hundred years.

This sneering, anti-Christian judge is of a piece with the Prime Minister of Canada – yes, with you, Jean-Joseph – who, at the time of the Papal condemnation of homosexuality as recently as in September 2003, declared yourself a Catholic, and yet you were going to vote in favour of the your Bill to recognize and to legalize the marriage of two people of the same sex.

Just three years previously the House of Commons, led by the Government, and by you as the Head of Government, had voted overwhelmingly in favour of marriage as being a union exclusively of a man and a woman.

What a turnabout! What treachery! What moral perversion! What brought about this reversion? Apart from family influence, and apart from a calculation of the votes involved, in your own statement you made a clear distinction between you, Jean-Joseph, the avowed Roman Catholic, and you, Jean-Joseph, the Liberal politician. That seems to be the sole piece of consistency in your political life – apart from your constant desire to make a fortune. It is that, on the one hand, you have condemned members of the Canadian Alliance for bringing their religious convictions into their political lives and their policies, and, on the other, your facility for divorcing your (apparent) religious beliefs from your political practices.

You accept and encourage immigrant Canadians to pursue their religious practices and beliefs, whether they be Muslims, Hindus, Sikhs, Buddhists or Shintu, and fully expect them to act in public according to the tenets of their faith. Yet you do not hesitate to condemn and ridicule Christians who do the same. What an enlightening spectacle you present – a 'Catholic' prime minister doing his best to undermine Christian ethics! And pray tell why you encourage Muslims and Sikhs to immigrate to Canada, when they alone of religious faiths produce the most violent fanatics and the most extreme terrorists?

For my part, – and I dare claim to speak for all right-thinking Canadians – I prefer a political candidate, and a minister of the Crown, to be consistent. If you say a thing, you believe it, and you will act accordingly. If you say you are a Christian, you must act as if you understood Christian ethics, and acted accordingly. In your case, Jean–Joseph, you say one thing and do another. But, you know something? We, the Canadian people, no longer expect anything else of you. You say you are a

Catholic; the Pope declares the Catholic position vis-à-vis, for example, the homosexual act; and you introduce a bill in Parliament that recognizes the marriage of same-sex couples. Not only have you betrayed your own position of three years ago: you have defied your own spiritual leader. You have taken the side of the Temporal against the Spiritual. Which is right. But don't also claim to be a Catholic. You have not only betrayed your Party and your promises: you have been a traitor to the Canadian people. You are Pilate! If Christ were to return during your administration, you would be the first to accuse him and to condemn him. And when he was being carted off, you would be lurking in the shadows, muttering: "It wasn't my fault! I didn't do it! It was Radwanski who said it was OK Munson assured me Radwanski told him it was OK! Munson checked with Easter, who reassured him that Radwanski had promised him there would be no repercussions, and that Munson would deny everything and send the evil media off on a wild goose chase...until *the enemy* cottoned on and we could concoct some other tale."

And what of the Jews? Why, you are anti-Jewish to the core, and anti-Israel, while pandering to the Arabs. Yes, the Arab states, run mostly by dictatorships. The historians of the subject point out that the Arab and other Muslim peoples have been ground down by their rulers and their faith for hundreds of years. And today, in Palestine, while the United Nations passes resolutions in favour of Palestine children who are targeted by Israel, Arafat and his terrorist regime have their schools filled with books depicting the most gruesome and satanic pictures and stories about the Israelis. The Jewish people, for their part, have enriched and ennobled mankind with their science and medicine, their learning and scholarship, their art and music and literature, and, yes, their humour, wherever and in whatever country they have been welcomed and sheltered.

You claim there is a divide between Church and State. This is Canada, not the United States. The Canadian Constitution recognizes no such separation. It is of your devising – for political ends. Look at the Preamble of your own Charter, and its recognition of God.

You scoff at members of the Alliance Party who openly declare their religious affiliations – as, in fact, you have. But they seem to believe that their religion requires them to act according to their beliefs. Does it matter whether the principles that underlie one's beliefs are religious or philosophical– or whatever? A person who acts and speaks according to his beliefs is a person of integrity. Do you know what 'integrity' means, Jean–Joseph? It means 'wholeness'. Wholeness of personality and character. You have proven by your own words, let alone by your own actions, that you are un–whole. You are unwholesome.

You are an enemy of democracy. You have proven yourself to be hostile to and destructive of democratic and parliamentary traditions, practices and principles. You are an enemy of the honourable principle of government by Cabinet. You are an enemy of justice: by your appointment of jurists to the Supreme Court of Canada who have made decisions consistent with your agenda of undermining the foundations of Canadian society, you reveal yourself to be the greatest threat to freedom in Canada.

In a word, you, Jean–Judas, have betrayed everything decent, honourable and principled in Canadian life. Even if your motives were other, you could not have done more to undermine the traditions and foundations of orderly, civilized Canadian society.

It is a matter of contempt that our bank notes are disfigured by the portraits of former politicians – the best of whom are politically and morally suspect – instead of being graced by the most illustrious of past explorers and Canadians, from Jacques Cartier on. Nothing in Canadian history more starkly illustrates the subservience of the Canadian people to government and authority. The dominance of the Liberal Party in Canadian history is due chiefly to the lack of independent thinking and independent action on the part of the mass of ordinary Canadians. The supineness of the whole of the present Liberal Cabinet and caucus merely reflects the apathy or ignorance of Canadian society. Take the gun registration fiasco. And I don't mean only its outrageous costs – over one billion dollars, when our Armed Forces people are being killed for lack of proper equipment. The day when your portrait appears on our Canadian currency – the face of corruption, evasion, nepotism, bribery, duplicity, bungling and irresponsibility – will be the day when the Western Provinces must kiss Eastern Canada goodbye in the name of a better future and honest government.

The individual is powerless to affect the fabric of civilized society, short of assassination. (But organized criminal gangs can do serious damage to a nation, as we in Canada know.) It is above all government, and politicians, who have the power and the means, and some the motives, to bring about lasting harm to their own people and country. And I'm not talking about Idi Amin and Mugabe and Saddam Hussein.

Your whole political life has been driven by ambition, lust and hatred. Ambition when not directed by principle is utterly corrupting. Your lust for power, wealth and control has been in evidence throughout your career. And your hatred for all things American and Anglophone has always been obvious.

Let me remind you that you swore oaths of office when you became a Member of Parliament, a Cabinet minister, and above all the Prime Minister. What oaths are they?

> I, ..., do solemnly and sincerely swear that I will truly and faithfully and to the best of my skill and knowledge execute and perform the duties that devolve upon me as a................ including the duty not to disclose or make known, without due authority in that behalf, any matter that comes to my knowledge by reason of my holding that office. So help me God.

Pretty mild stuff, that! So I leave it to later historians and biographers to decipher and analyse what is meant by "solemnly and sincerely swear"; by "truly and faithfully"; by "to the best of my skill and knowledge", and by "duties". But if these oaths are set beside your words and deeds, it would appear that you took the oaths with the firm intention of forswearing them as and when the situation demanded, according to your political requirement of the moment.

What now if we look at the words of our National Anthem? Why, you don't believe them, Jean–Joseph, no matter how hard you sing them. And you are of the kind who, the louder you sing the louder you lie through your teeth. I won't even bother to display all the words. Just to quote the phrase, "We stand on guard for thee", reveals you for what you are.

Then we have the statement on the Government web site defining the Mission and the Values of the Privy Council. The third of the four Values reads: "We believe that integrity, judgement and discretion are essential to achieving our mission." Our mission: shall I quote that too? It reads: "To serve Canada ... by providing the best non-partisan advice and support to the Prime Minister and Cabinet." Words fail me, where words, mere words, uttered without a care for their meaning or implied promises, are the stock-in-trade of you Liberals.

That you should still bear the title, the Right Honourable, is more than any decent, honest, patriotic and law–abiding Canadian can tolerate. The Earl of Rosebery once proclaimed that, "politics s an evil–smelling bog." You have spent forty years confirming that verdict. I would go further and say that, if Rosebery had been here to observe your performance as prime minister, his indictment would have been severer still. He would have crowned you the undisputed Baron of All Bogs, the Bogmaster of Quebec, the Tsar of Shawinigan Bogs.

Three centuries before Rosebery, a famous Englishman who had an English king beheaded, proclaimed before the Parliament of the day: "You have sat here too long for any good you have done. It is time that you were gone. I say to you, "In the name of God, be gone!"

I say to you, Jean–Joseph, in the name of decency and honesty, in the name of all faithful and loyal Canadians, "For God's sake, GO!"

POSTSCRIPT

The Political Parties

Canada is afflicted with four federal parties – without counting the ridiculous separatist Parti Québécois. They are the Progressive Conservative Party, the New Democratic Party, the Liberal Party, and the Canadian Alliance Party

The Progressive Conservative Party is the product of the amalgamation of the Conservative Party and the Progressive Party in 1942. Whether or not the people present at the conception and birth of this mule ever paused to think that 'progressive' and 'conservative' are contradictory and incompatible terms, the sad fact is that the wishy–washy outcome almost guaranteed generations of life in the wilderness. The fusion of the two parties was a repetition of the union of three protestant sects to form the United Church of Canada – with an equally ineffective series of compromises that resulted in the expulsion of much good doctrine and principle.

The New Democratic Party is a socialist party. Its tenets are grounded in a hatred and fear of capitalism and big business, and, in the latter days, of globalization; and in its identification with and promotion of the labour movement. It is destined to remain a rump in Parliament, if only for the reasons that it has a narrow, and narrow-minded, electoral base, and that it is incapable of explaining how the nation would create and acquire its wealth without the enterprise, research and development that are the hallmarks of freedom of trade and capital. To think otherwise is to hold up as examples of progress the model economies of Cuba, Zimbabwe, and the imploded Soviet Union. Or even of pre-Thatcher Britain!

On the other hand, it is perhaps not surprising that many ministers of the cloth are to be found within its ranks, and it is to their great credit that they are the authors of the social doctrine that no one in Canada need ever go in want of food, shelter and clothing. This doctrine is an article of Christian teaching. But, alas, the downside of this doctrine is hugely destructive. For where once Christian ethics were a personal and neighbourhood spur to action, the State has seen fit to interfere and has cast the individual aside. So that whereas in the Great Depression everyone was ready to help his neighbour in want, today no one will stop his car and offer a lift to an old person standing in the rain at a bus stop; or even call the police from the safety of their home when they hear, or even see, a helpless person being attacked outside their window.

The Liberal Party of Canada is a thieving magpie. Long ago it abandoned its traditional and honourable philosophy and principles in favour of the simple doctrine as enunciated in the terse commandment: Thou shalt get elected, and stay elected. This is the sole Liberal mantra – followed by its corollary: Thou shalt swear fealty to the Leader. The consequences of this edict are that the liberals lie, cheat and steal during elections, and continue to lie, cheat and steal thereafter. They will promise the earth, and when it is pointed out to them that hey have not delivered a bucketful of soil let alone the earth, they wax indignant and explain, like a kindergarten teacher to a wayward and uncomprehending child, that they had never promised anything of the sort, that obviously you weren't paying attention, and that they could not possibly have made such a promise when doing so would commit them to an action in the future when they could not know what Canadians' needs would be then.

Having forsaken their former principles, the Liberals, finding themselves elected by a gullible electorate, then have to cast about for some plausible policies to implement. Generally they look no farther than to the Opposition parties. Then Liberals plunder their ideas, test them in the wind of public opinion, and if the polls seem favourable, they purloin them and dress them up as their own. That is why Liberal policies and practices span the gamut of the political colours, from the bright red of socialist meddling, control and regulation, to the deep blue of conservative capitalism. Frequently they clash, and there follows an almighty snafu of contradiction, conflicting interests and incompatibility, with the concomitant ministerial and bureaucratic bungling, evasion and finger–pointing. Today it is difficult to tell the Liberals and NDPers apart. Perhaps one test is this: that if Chrétien switched sides, he would elevate the intellectual calibre of both parties at a stroke.

Pundits have a habit of saying that Canadians deserve better that what the Liberals give them. Rubbish. Canadians have brought it upon themselves and have no one to blame but themselves.

The Canadian Alliance Party, like its predecessor the Reform Party of Canada, is an attempt to create a true conservative party in place of the current PC Party, which has gone soft and is in dissolution. The Alliance, which is largely a protest party with its origin and its roots in Western Canada, will go nowhere without winning over central Canada to its doctrine. With new leadership in both parties, an amalgamation of the two into one true Conservative Party of Canada with a broad national appeal promises the sole hope of creating a strong and united Opposition in Parliament to a discredited and morally bankrupt Liberal government. If it never forms the government, an effective opposition is as vital to a healthy democracy as is an effective government.

Conservatism stands for nothing if it does not stand for Freedom, Tradition, Democracy, Responsibility, and a Humane Capitalism. These values imply that, if a revivified and renewed Canadian Conservative Party comes into being, much of the work of the past twenty years will have to be undone or redone. Many things come to mind. Here are two. The first is the proposed flat tax. A flat tax would do away with all the grave inequities currently made possible by the Liberal

administrators of the Income Tax Act in favour
of the wealthy and influential. It would also
result in the elimination of thousands of Civil
Service positions filled by men and women who
would then be released to take up productive
employment in the private sector. It would also,
of course, liberate thousands of tax accountants
and lawyers from their lucrative servitude.

The second is the infamous Liberal
doctrine of political correctness. Political
correctness is, as we have seen, an invasive and
surreptitious social evil designed by devious
politicians and bureaucrats with the intent of
stifling freedom of thought and expression, and
of inhibiting open discussion of controversial
questions, no matter how important they are.
Canadians are threatened with criminal
prosecution at the merest hint that something
they say might offend the sensibilities of some
minority individual or group. Example? A
Canadian watched his neighbour, an immigrant
from the Near East, beating a rug and asked
jokingly: "What's the matter? Won't it start?"
The new Canadian laid a complaint against him
with the provincial Human Rights Commission,
whose Liberal-appointed members found him
guilty of some spurious offence against some
so-called manufactured human right.
Canadians have to bend the knee to immigrants

and to watch their words in their own home. Not the least aspect of Chrétien's legacy is this *mentalité minoritaire,* typical of a small town Québécois who sides with minorities against the majority, because he is perverted by an inferiority complex. Chrétien, inferiority complex? You bet! Ask the psychiatrist. That is, the non–Liberal ones.

Are Canadians afraid of FREEDOM? Are they afraid to stand up for themselves, to fight their own battles, to refuse handouts and freebies, until they reach the point, and recognize the point, of being able to look after themselves? You know what disgusts decent people? They are all in favour of helping the poor and the weak, until they can begin to look after themselves. But when decent hardworking Canadians hear about privileged people and millionaire socialists, applying for and accepting fat grants for so called research, Canadians must be hard put to it to refrain from launching a rocket at the Canadian Social Sciences and Humanities Research Council. Or the Liberal Government.

Or are Canadians satisfied with the nanny state, with being looked after from the cradle to the grave, especially by people who have to have an Ethics Counsellor because they don't know the difference between right and wrong?

Political correctness is a subversive ideology that must be crushed. Let us reiterate that clarion call to arms of Voltaire in the name of Liberty: *"Écrasez l'infâme!"*

Postscript. This is not good enough. More must be said. Political correctness is more than a duplicitous stratagem: it is a grotesque doctrine subversive of the most fundamental right of all rights in a supposedly free and democratic country, that of the right to freedom of speech and expression. Its energetic promotion by you and your government is of a piece with all your efforts to restrict Canadians' basic freedoms. Canada is no longer a free country, and in the pursuit of your agenda to impose restrictions you have proven yourself to be anti-Canadian. And your anti-Canadianism is one facet of your *mentalité québécoise,* which is steeped in authoritarianism and anti-English bile.

Your policy of political correctness -- or, in fittter words, political corruptness -- favours people of minority races, and protects them against people of the majority from any remark that they, the minority, might infer as being a slur. And, of course, the ultimate minority is the people of Quebec. NO, that is not correct: not the people of Quebec, but the French-speaking people of Quebec. After all, it was your government --or rather you personally -- who decided that you would not appeal the ruling of the Supreme Court of Canada that the Quebec Official Languages Act was unconstitutional, and therefore illegal.

The latest manifestation of this policy of yours to suppress freedom of speech and expression whenever a minority bellowed: "Racism!" or some other equally criminal remark, comes from some subversive called Jean Augustine. It appears that a sports commentator on CBC radio observed with some scorn that in hockey "the only players who wore visors on their helmets were Europeans and French guys." The commentator, Don Cherry, did not say "Quebec guys": he said "French guys". Nevertheless, an inquisition was launched by Canada's Official Languages Commissioner, the CBC Ombudsman, and the Canadian Broadcast Standards Council.. Not to be outdone, the infamous Jean Augustine, who glories in the office of Junior Minister for Multiculturalism, issued this statement: "The government will not tolerate statements that create dissonance in our society." We may interpret that statement as implying by "our society", "Quebec society", not "Canadian society". What has Prime Minister Paul Martin to say? So far he has been mum -- as on all controversial and substantive issues.

Most Canadians will probably hear the words "not tolerate ... dissonance in our society" and think of the left wing tyrannies, Stalin's communist Soviet Union or Hitler's nazi Germany. (Rather than Mussolini's right wing fascist movement, which was relatively benign.)

This brings us in full circle back to the Prime Minister's Office. It is a matter of both wonderment and alarm that this office has never attracted the attention of the press that it calls for. It is the symbol and instrument of all the evils and wrongs we have catalogued. It is the subversive agency of the diminution or debasement of both Parliament and Cabinet. It is the repository of a power conferred on it solely by the Prime Minister, and in constitutional terms it is illegitimate, if nothing worse.

Let us attempt to summarize its aims and functions:

the concentration of political power in a few hands;

a compliant centrally-organized bureaucracy;

a system of tightly overseen political control over all important appointments, including even the anti-democratic measure of approving or disapproving candidates for election to Parliament;

the promotion and imposition of a so-called social democracy from above;

the readiness to put ends before the means used to achieve them;

the setting of various sections and components of society against each other on the basis of religion, race, language and region.

Now it happens by an extraordinary coincidence that these are the very aims of Leninism-Stalinism. It is also a strange coincidence that Trudeau's ill-conceived National Energy Plan (NEP) is an echo of the Soviet New Economic Plan (NEP).

But these seeming parallels must not be pursued too far, for we must remember that in Canada we still enjoy some freedoms, and periodical elections, even though the Liberal Government has tried on numerous occasions to stifle freedom of speech.

Three Principles

The political history of every nation that belongs to what is called Western Civilization, whose governments are elected in free elections, demonstrates that no Opposition party has ever won an election.

The manifold task, and objective, of the Opposition is threefold.

It must at all times present a united face before the world. There may be rumours, or even leaks, of disagreement and division within its ranks. That is not only inevitable: it is not to be feared. The free exchange of ideas among people who are essentially likeminded is to be welcomed by all who cherish freedom of speech and expression above all freedoms. For they know that thinking minds need to rub up against each other to give off sparks of truth. But once they have rubbed enough, they must close ranks about an agreed position.

The Opposition must, over time, present to Parliament and the Great Public whose servants, not masters, they hope to become, a coherent set of principles and policies that seek to accomplish two things:

i) to convince the People that their policies are sound, reasoned, and designed to meet the needs of the times; and

ii) to offer a responsible and plausible alternative to the policies being pursued by the

Government of the day, and to the moral character of the Government.

It must hold the Government of the day accountable for both its policies and its policy vacuums, as judged in the light of its own policies; and it must constantly hold the feet of the individual Ministers of the Crown to the fire, in assessing the performance of their duties and their failures. Above all, the Opposition must never let up in its vigilance in exposing and condemning all signs of corruption, nepotism, patronage and other forms of wrongdoing by governing politicians tempted to abuse their power.

If no Opposition ever won an election, the corollary is that elections are lost, not won. That being the case, it stands that elections are lost, and lost by the Government in office at the time of the election. The reasons may be many. I leave it to our political philosophers – whom I prefer over our academic political "scientists' – to analyze the election results over the past hundred years. In recent times, in Canada, just think Diefenbaker, Turner, Trudeau, Campbell, Mulroney and you will understand what I mean. Of course in the Provinces, the examples are even more numerous and just as striking.

If political calculation can be made into a principle, it may be attempted in these terms. No party or government should ever calculate the public reaction to a proposed policy or measure. That is the way of demagogues and ideologues. A Government should formulate a policy, then persuade the public of its necessity.

A little calculation is needed, however, especially by a party in opposition, in order to steer clear of highly controversial issues which, if announced without previous study, would risk alienating voters. It is essential that such matters be discussed freely and openly in caucus, where it will be decided which issues fall under that rubric. Why stir up a potential hornet's nest by re-opening delicate issues – no matter how publicly important they are – when there are so many other vital reforms and public policies that are crying aloud for action?

On the other hand, matters of public policy should not be swept under the rug or silenced for good just because they are controversial or divisive. There may be a time and an occasion to re-introduce into public debate questions like capital punishment, abortion, homosexual unions, compulsory trade union dues etc. When that time and that occasion are judged to be ripe, the debate should be opened in the public forum, and not in such a manner that it appears to be government- or party-sponsored.

APPENDIX

The decision in the litigation between M. François Beaudoin and the Government of Canada, brought by the former to have restored his pension and severance payments after his dismissal as president of the Business Development Bank of Canada, was brought down by Justice André Denis in the Quebec Superior Court on February 6th. What follows is an abridged version of the report that was published in the *National Post* of February 7th.

"A Quebec Superior Court judge ruled yesterday that François Beaudoin, ... was the apparent victim of a political vendetta orchestrated by friends of Jean Chrétien, the former prime minister." Judge André Denis'(s) decision, which orders the federal government bank to make pension and severance payments it had withheld from Mr. Beaudoin, completely vindicates Mr. Beaudoin while indicting the BDC's conduct. Beaudoin was abruptly let go in 1999 after falling out of favour with Michel Vennat, a friend of Mr. Chrétien, who had recently been named chairman of the BDC board of directors. Mr. Beaudoin suspected he was being punished for raising questions about a $615,000 loan to the Auberge Grand'Mère. Mr. Chrétien sold the hotel to Shawinigan businessman Yvon Duhaime in 1993 and personally pressured Mr. Beaudoin to approve the loan, even though Mr. Duhaime was ineligible for the assistance. After initially agreeing in September, 1999, to honour Mr. Beaudoin's $245,000 severance package and $200,000 a year pension, the bank reneged, claiming Mr. Beaudoin had used bank goods and services for his personal gain while president. Judge Denis rejected that charge and identified Jean Carle, Mr. Chrétien's former director of operations who was named a vice-president at the BDC in March 1998. as 'the prime organizer" of the effort to discredit Mr. Beaudoin. "Mr. Vennat and Mr. Carle are personal friends of the Prime Minister, and that is their right;' the judge wrote. "But the file of the Auberge Grand'Mère and the media coverage surrounding it gave Mr. Beaudoin the impression that he was victim of a vendetta that went beyond the simple study of his performance as president of a Crown corporation.... The ferocity, even malice, with which he was treated during this whole affair certainly allows him to think what he did."

Addressing warrants obtained by the bank in 2001 to search Mr. Beaudoin's home, his cottage and his office for BDC documents, Judge Denis again raised the question of a vendetta. He noted the searches, which he called "a disgrace," came as pressure was mounting on Mr. Chrétien over what had become known as Shawinigate. "In fact, the entire operation reinforces in an impartial observer the impression of a vendena orchestrated by the BDC against Mr. Beaudoin;" he wrote. "The media and the parliamentry opposition were pursuing the prime minister on the Auberge Grand'Mère file. That is their constitutional right in our parliamentary and judicial system."

Speaking to reporters yesterday at the offices of his lawyer, Mr. Beaudoin urged Paul Martin, Mr. Chrétien's successor, to take the necessary steps to shield the bank from political interference. 'I think it's a good institution. I think it should not be politicized;' he said. 'I think Mr. Martin should look at the steps that are required to depoliticize a bank that is lending money. You don't mix politics and money. This is a bad recipe.'

Mr. Beaudoin, who spoke about the controversial loan with Mr. Chrétien on three occasions in 1996 and 1997, said the former

prime minister did not disclose that he was still
owed money by the owners of the golf club
adjacent to the hotel. Mr. Chrétien had sold his
stake in the golf club in 1993 but did not
receive full payment until 1999. 'The Prime
Minister is the one who started the process
when he first called me about this loan. The
issue that he raised was the fact that he had no
direct or indirect involvement in the Auberge or
in the golf club;' Mr. Beaudoin said. 'In
retrospect, I think this comment lacked
objectivity because there were facts which we
were not aware of. If I had known that he had
this involvement, direct or indirect, I would have
acted differently.' Mr. Chrétien's assistant in his
Montreal law office said he was out of the
country yesterday and unavailable for comment.
Guy Beaudry, vice-president corporate affairs
for the BDC, said the bank has not ruled out an
appeal, despite Judge Denis'(s) suggestion that
it is time to "raise the white flag."

Reading from a prepared statement, Mr.
Beaudry said: 'The bank believed in the
rightness of its cause and is considering its
options.' He declined additional comment and
refused to say how much public money was
spent in the proceedings against Mr. Beaudoin.
In addition to the legal fees for the lengthy trial,
the BDC commissioned a forensic audit by

KPMG - which Judge Denis said was so flawed he could not consider it as evidence - and hired a criminal lawyer in a failed effort to push for criminal charges after the Crown had decided against charging Mr. Beaudoin. (The RCMP first investigated after Mr. Vennat, who is now bank president, complained directly to RCMP Commissioner Giullano Zaccardelli.) Doug Mitchell, Mr. Beaudoin's lawyer, estimated that BDC's bill for the case is 'millions of dollars.'

'Some of Judge Denis'(s) harshest criticism was reserved for Mr. Carle, who left the bank in 2000. Mr. Carle had testified that he knew of no link between the Auberge Grand'Mère and Mr. Chrétien, aside from the fact the inn was located in the former prime minister's riding. "The court gives no credibility to this witness, who was visibly nervous during his entire testimony, gave evasive if not downright false answers and was contradicted by other witnesses;" the judge wrote. He said Mr. Carle acted as if the prime minister was the sole shareholder in the BDC. "You no longer seek, as a Crown corporation, to give the straight goods to the media, nor to say the truth, but simply repeat the position of the Prime Minister's Office;" Judge Denis wrote. He also concluded that Mr. Vennat's credibility was "largely undermined" by contradictory testimony from other witnesses. <u>Commentary</u>. We have few comments to make, but they are vital, if obvious. Messrs Vennat and Carle, if we interpret correctly the opinions of the eminent judge, committed perjury. If the new Attorney-General reaches that conclusion, they should be charged with that criminal offence, and removed from their offices in the meantime. Since Vennat and Carle are "personal friends" of Chrétien, and acted on his behalf – and clearly did not act without his approval, either tacit or expres – legal opinion should be sought as to whether criminal proceedings should be brought against Chrétien. At the very least, Vennat and Carle have substantiated every allegation of corruption made against Chrétien in these pages. Finally, if the present government decides to appeal, it will be with Mr. Martin's approval; and such approval would plant Mr. Martin squarely in an evil camp.

For a more comprehensive view of
Canada today, the reader should
visit the website

www.letter-from-canada.org

About the Author

The author served for twelve years in the Royal Air Force, as an armourer and pilot, then went to Oxford and took an honours degree in Modern Languages. He immigrated to Canada and served in the Royal Canadian Air Force as a security/intelligence officer for five years before resigning his commission to enter university teaching. He took his PhD at Stanford, and taught French Literature for thirty-one years and retired to the West Coast in 1990, where he busies himself writing.

Canada has been good to him, and he hopes he has given something in return. He has constantly had before him these words of Albert Camus: "No, I do not love my country, if not loving means denouncing what is unjust in the thing we love, if it means that what we love should come up to the noblest conception we have of it."

It is easy to praise what is good in a person and country; and praise shows the capacity for useful discrimination, being also educational. But criticism is also essential, if it is constructive, if it leads to the exposure of injustices and the correction of vices.

In this booklet the author has not pulled any punches in his condemnation of Jean Chrétien's record. But he reserves a special contempt for Chrétien's Cabinet and Liberal caucus, who could have stopped Chrétien in his tracks at any time, but took the dishonourable path of clinging to their comfortable offices and fat pensions and vaporous celebrity.

The author is also saddened by the indefinite prospect of so many thousands of his fellow Canadians displaying political naiveté and poor political judgement election after election. Do our schools do nothing to train our young people to think for themselves and to form their judgement?

Jack Dixon is the author of the acclaimed book, *The Battle of Britain: Victory and Defeat* (Woodfield Publishing, 2003).

ISBN 141202166-9